with love to Ivy !!.

Minelle Mahtani

MAY IT
HAVE
A HAPPY
ENDING

*A memoir of finding my voice
as my mother lost hers*

Doubleday Canada

Doubleday Canada and colophon are registered trademarks of Penguin Random House Canada Limited

Library and Archives Canada Cataloguing in Publication

Title: May it have a happy ending: a memoir / Minelle Mahtani.
Names: Mahtani, Minelle, 1971- author.
Identifiers: Canadiana (print) 20240327144 | Canadiana (ebook) 20240327276 |
ISBN 9780385675208 (hardcover) | ISBN 9780385675215 (EPUB)
Subjects: LCSH: Mahtani, Minelle, 1971- | LCSH: Mahtani, Minelle, 1971- — Family. |
LCSH: Mahtani, Minelle, 1971- — Health. | LCSH: Mothers and daughters —
Canada — Biography. | LCGFT: Autobiographies.
Classification: LCC HQ755.86 .M34 2024 | DDC 306.874/3092 — dc23

Some names and identifying characteristics have been changed to protect individuals' privacy, and some events have been collapsed and re-arranged slightly.

Jacket design: Talia Abramson
Jacket art: (flower) Tatiana, (saree) jayant khedekar, (carpet) andrei_77, all Adobe Stock; (moon) Mike Petrucci / Unsplash; (bird) denisko / Getty Images; (feather) mckenna71 / Shutterstock
Interior images: illustrations by Daisy Osberg; (title page) Gluiki/Getty Images; (dingbat) zolotons/Adobe Stock
Typesetting: Daniella Zanchetta
Permissions: Portions of this work were originally published in
carte blanche, Maisonneuve, Rigorous, The Walrus and *Voices from the Fold.*
Additional permissions listed on page 321.

Printed in Canada

Published in Canada by Doubleday Canada,
a division of Penguin Random House Canada Limited

www.penguinrandomhouse.ca

10 9 8 7 6 5 4 3 2 1

To Ing Wong-Ward—
For always asking me the right questions.

THIS BOOK IS A PRAYER.

"darling,
you feel heavy
because you are
too full of truth.

open your mouth more.
let the truth exist
somewhere other than
inside your body."

— DELLA HICKS-WILSON, *Small Cures*

CONTENTS

Prologue, 1

Part One: SILENCE

Part Two: SOUND

Part Three: THE MOTHER VOICE AS STRESS RELIEF

Part Four: QUESTIONS AND ANSWERS

Part Five: NUMBERS AND SIGNS

Part Six: DEATH IS NOT THE OPPOSITE OF LIFE

Part Seven: JOY

Inside Nature's Haven Naturopathics, I was enveloped by the musty, lingering scent of aging grains and essential oils. It felt safe and inviting, the aroma reminiscent of the spice cupboards of my childhood: cumin, coriander and cloves. I breathed in, deeply comforted, if only for that moment.

The owner of the store, Owen, had long hair and warm eyes. He locked the front door and placed a dilapidated sign in the window: *Back in five minutes*. Leaning over my mother as she sat on a wooden stool, he said he wanted to try something. He started to rub her shoulders gently.

"Get it out, Farideh," he said quietly. "Get it all out. Scream. Aren't you mad that you have tongue cancer?"

Tears rolled down my face. "Mom, please."

It was the fall of 2015. I had taken a leave from hosting my radio show in Vancouver to drive my mother to various appointments in Toronto. Always another doctor's appointment. On this day, I was trying something different in the hopes that this shop would offer us a magic elixir. Grasping beyond the broken bureaucracy of the health care system.

"Try, try, Mom. Please."

I could feel all the things she wanted to say. Her hands trembled in mine. She tried to scream. Nothing. Suddenly and slightly, a slow, piercing howl emerged from her mouth, like no other sound I had ever heard. I thought of the word *keen*. I stood beside her, shocked into silence. How could that sound — that guttural wail — come from her wounded body, her body that could no longer speak?

I thought of Rita Wong's poem "reconnaissance":

habitual placement of the tongue changes the mouth.
when the tongue is still, are you
quiet enough to hear the dead?
quiet enough to hear the land stifled beneath massive
concrete? quiet enough to hear the beautiful, poisoned
ancestors surfacing from your diaphragm?

I thought about all the stories of my ancestors, now buried in my mother's mouth.

PART ONE

SILENCE

"Silence properly understood is not merely a lack of sound, nor is it an absence . . . silence only has presence as silence because it points to something beyond itself, which throws the silence into relief. Silence and speech too are mutually reliant on each other for meaning."

— SUSAN BICKFORD, *The Dissonance of Democracy*

How It Begins

This is a story about how I gained a voice when my mom was losing hers. But this is not the entire story, of course. No story ever is. Every story is also another story, another three, or four, or five.

And every silence is a story too.

This story is also about the risks we take in trying to render silences obsolete. It is about the damage that silence does to the body. I want to speak to you about that deafening power of silence.

And while this is a story about the loss of a loved one, it is also a story about many kinds of loss: the loss of a job, the loss of a city and the loss of a life-world.

Of course, it is also about the gain of a partner and a little boy, but this is a false arithmetic of intimacies — they are not emotionally equivalent nor could they ever be.

And so how to begin this story of many stories, with its multiple beginnings?

Here is one way.

The story I am about to tell you starts with my own mouth, just as it ended with hers.

Since moving to Vancouver two weeks before, in early days of 2015, I had noticed that when I looked very closely, my face resembled a lopsided figure in a Picasso painting, the left side of my lip curling ever so slightly downward, as if forced into a half frown. Not only that, but my left hand had started trembling, my fingers like a frantic bird as I tried to serve dinner to my two-year-old son, Cole, and partner, Bruce — the silver serving spoon clattering to the kitchen floor one night, just out of my grasp. Another evening, I felt a foreign numbness in my left foot as I struggled to put on a pair of woollen socks.

It was only after heaving my left leg out of bed with a heavy grunt one morning, the limb uncompromising, that I could no longer lie to myself.

I crept out at the first sign of daylight, leaving Bruce and Cole undisturbed, both of them lightly snoring, and limped to the bus stop.

The ER doctor peered into my face and said, "Has your eye always drooped like that, a little to the left?"

I wanted to say *No, this is new.* But that was not the truth.

The truth is that I have always been uneven.

Ten years earlier, when I was thirty-four, a hairdresser at a salon on Bond Street at Broadway in New York City had scrutinized my scalp. "Your hair grows unevenly," she'd said. "It's strong on one side, very thin on the other." I'd peered closer, pretending I didn't already know. When I was seven, playing in the bathtub, I'd noticed that the hair on my body grew differently on one side, leg hair thicker on the left than the right. When puberty hit, it was even more prominent.

So, you see: off balance, off-kilter. Never reaching equilibrium.

Mixed race: the oxymoron. Two opposites. Right? Indian, Iranian. Muslim, Hindu. My entire life has been about keeping score. Two sides against each other. Wins, losses. Ups, downs.

I needed a win now. I was on a losing streak. My body was failing me.

Shivering in that hospital room, my hand still shaking, the doctor shelling me with poisoned questions, I chose to dodge, weave, evade. *How long has the numbness been there, the tingling, the droop?* More light blinding my eyes, repeated requests to follow the physician's finger with my gaze. *When did you notice the limp?*

Then the physician's pronouncement: "I think you may have had a mini-stroke."

The stench of ammonia wafted over me. My stomach churned. We had packed up our apartment in Toronto two weeks earlier. We had moved so that we could be together as a family in one place, no longer doing long distance. Well-meaning friends had approached me with such sincere concern: Did I really want to give up so much? My job at the university? My shiny new condo at Spadina and Bloor? My mother nearby? Was I convinced that I was taking the right path? Then, too, I had evaded the questions. I could not have known the future: that in mere months, my formerly vibrant and vital mother would be in a palliative care hospital bed in Markham Stouffville Hospital.

Since arriving in Vancouver, any buoyancy I'd felt at a fresh start had been replaced with dread. While Cole was in daycare and Bruce at work at the university, I was alone in our cramped sublet. I had no job, and I was feeling untethered. What had I done in the name of love? In jettisoning all that I knew for this one person, these two people.

My body was speaking what I refused to voice.

My First Words

Or maybe the story starts here:

I was in grade two, six years old. An awkward, bucktoothed little girl, very conscious of my ungainly appearance. I was shy. Kept to myself. A bookworm. I sat cross-legged on the floor, listening to my teacher read a story. I don't remember its name.

One of my classmates sat close to me. Now, his name I still remember.

He hissed at me. I was at first flattered, thinking it was a gesture of affection. But then I looked at his face. His face was red. He spat something out of his mouth — a word I did not recognize. I had no idea what this word meant. But I knew from his tone that it wasn't a compliment.

I returned home and found my mother brushing her long, burnished brown hair at her vanity. I asked, "Mom, what does *tigger* mean? Am I one?"

Before I could read her face, she turned away from me, rushed behind her bedroom door.

"Mommy? What does the word mean?"

Even now I remember the sound of her sobbing, her shudders of breath.

"Mommy? I'm sorry. I'm sorry! I didn't mean it."

Many years later, as a scholar studying multiraciality, I would write about the phenomenon of cocooning: mixed race children tend not to share their racist experiences with their parents for fear of upsetting them.

The first of many mixed race lessons: keep quiet when you're humiliated — to protect yourself, and the people you love.

An Opportunity

That chilly morning in the ER, the doctor tried to hand me a sheaf of papers. Referrals for a battery of tests: an MRI, a CT scan. But before she could, the sheets scattered to the cold linoleum floor like dry, cracked autumn leaves. I wanted to leave the papers there, to be swallowed by the earth, but I hurriedly bent to gather them to my chest.

She said, "I don't want to scare you, but I'd also like to send you to the MS clinic."

I did not allow this choice bit of information to settle into my bones. I left it on the surface of my skin, where it would sit uncomfortably for some time.

I staggered home. Upon arrival, my little boy whined for cereal. My partner looked at me with uncertainty. *How did it go?*

My expression: *I don't know, honey.*

My hand, still trembling.

Bruce took our son to daycare an hour later, strapped safely into his bike seat. I sat quietly at the kitchen table. The sun was pouring in and my laptop was open before me, but I was not in a writing mood. Friends had suggested I use this time as a mini-sabbatical, to get some academic writing done. But I could feel it: the depression that had dogged me my entire life was returning. I didn't want to do anything except watch Netflix. Years ago, over steaming lattes, my mentor Sherene had wryly told me that for me to get tenure, I needed to have triple the publications that white feminist scholars did. So I wrote. I published twenty-three articles. I put out two books with my name on the cover. Now, I was tired.

My leg, still shaking.

I closed my laptop and limped to the water. The ocean was mere minutes away. I sat on a bench at the top of the hill at Vine and 4th Avenue in Kitsilano and stared flatly at the skyline, at where the water met the mountains.

What the hell was I doing?

I had travelled around the globe for my career: first by pursuing a PhD in London (grey, wet, beautiful Bloomsbury Square), followed by a semester in Chapel Hill, North Carolina (a crumbling ante-bellum mansion with a wraparound porch and seemingly endless sunny autumn days, happily surrounded by a teetering mountain of books) for a postdoctoral fellowship at Duke, then the coveted teaching job at the New School in Greenwich Village, Manhattan (that glorious find of an apartment on the second floor of a brown-stone in Cobble Hill — with bright red geraniums bookending the clay-coloured stoop; that time of commutes on the F train at sunset and luscious steak frites at Bar Tabac, my treat to myself after teaching "Space, Race and Gender" on Wednesday nights), capped, finally, by a tenure-track offer in Toronto (the very place I had started in so many years ago). I had chosen to give all this up to follow my part-ner to Vancouver, where his job was. I had taken a leave of absence from the university in Toronto. I hadn't wanted to give up my job when there was so much uncertainty in the balance. I didn't know if I'd return, or what would come next.

Untethered, trembling.

And then I got the phone call.

A friend in journalism, Kirk, told me that a new radio station, Roundhouse, was opening up in Vancouver — a commercial station with a community feel. He was taking on the drive-in show in the morning. There was a slot for another show between ten and twelve, and he wanted to recommend me for the job of radio host. I could bring my politics to it — talk about race if I wanted to. Did I want to audition?

Before my time in academia, I had worked in television production but behind the scenes. I had no experience hosting. I had never once wanted to be on camera. That's not to say it wasn't floated in my direction. *The way you look, Minelle, you could be whatever the viewer thinks you are — you could be Algerian! Italian! Possibly Portuguese!* This was always said with such energy, as if no one could resist its sparkly, seductive pull. I knew this game and had been forced to play it for years.

I didn't want to be in front of the camera, and I wasn't sure I was cut out to host radio either. But then I remembered my laptop at the apartment. The academic journal article reviews I was ignoring. My quivering limb. I felt empty and unmoored. I told my friend I would think about it.

The next phone call was to my mother. My mother, with whom I checked in about almost everything: how much *haldi* I should stir into warm milk when I have a sore throat; whether this J.Crew shirt goes with those jeans; which *dua* I should say when I'm feeling particularly low.

"Mom?"

As always, she was delighted to hear from me, as if my voice was the only one that mattered. "Muni! I miss you!"

Part of me wants to tell you here, in muted tones, about the sound of her voice, her accent. Part of me wants to tell you everything. But right now, I cannot — it's too hard for me to share this detail, this primary intimacy, with someone I barely know. Maybe I'll share it with you later after we get to know each other a little better. But for now, you'll just have to imagine.

"Muni! How are you doing, *junam*? How is Vancouver?"

I breathlessly told her about the opportunity. "What do you think?" I asked hesitantly.

There was no hesitation on her part. "You must do it, Muni! You must!" Her excitement burbled through her words. "Why not meet with the man doing the hiring and find out more? It can't hurt, right, Muni?"

Her enthusiasm made me smile. I scanned the horizon again where the sky and sand collided and thought, *Yes. Yes, I will try.* Because I had always listened to her.

Something I Loved about Her

I was rushing home for lunch, my grade-four report card fresh in my hands. My younger brother, Reza, and I usually ate lunch at home; Mom always left a meal for us in the fridge. But today, Ray was eating at school, so I was coming home alone. I planned to leave the report card on the dining table for Mom to see when she came home that night. But when I barged through the door, there she was, taking off her alligator pumps in the vestibule, rubbing her feet. (She was always rubbing her feet. Even when she was at work. And she always wore heels — she had a head-to-toe attention to detail that made everything beautiful.) I was surprised. Typically, she was at her Montessori school at this time. I remember she wore a high-necked silk blouse, an A-line skirt. Her makeup perfectly applied. Coral-pink lipstick.

She greeted me lovingly, as she always did; always so happy to see me, as if it were the first time after a long time.

I told her I got my report card. Her face was still for a moment. I handed it over with some reluctance. I hadn't read it yet.

She opened the manila envelope with deep seriousness, then her deathly expression turned joyful.

"*Mashallah, beti* — all A's! I am so proud of you!"

She squealed and lifted me up, startling me, swinging me around wildly in our hallway constrained by jackets and hockey sticks and basketballs and umbrellas. She didn't hear the thwack of my skull up against the doorknob, she didn't feel what I felt, too caught up in her revelry.

She put me down and she was busy staring at the report card again, tracing it gently with her fingers, quietly reading the comments, scarcely audible, as if they were a prayer she was reciting to herself. I surreptitiously rubbed the bump on my head, hoping she wouldn't notice. It started to bleed, but only a little.

After she died, I found the report card and rubbed the spot on my head again.

The bump was long gone, of course, but the body remembers.

When you tell your cousin Anise this story many years later, he looks at you and says,

"That sounds like a reason you hated her, not loved her."

You stop, startled.

You couldn't see the difference.

You still can't.

Something I Hated about Her

Before almost every weekend outing to see relatives and friends, she used to chase me around the house with an Avon rouge stick, its shade a sickly orange-red, so wrong for my skin colour, but perfect for hers. Up and down our moss-green carpeted stairs we'd go, like we were partners in some comedy routine, a Brown Abbott and Costello.

"Muni, please put this on! You look so pale! You need some colour on your cheeks!"

Her face, a canvas of perfection, thanks to years of cosmetology school. Didn't I tell you how beautiful she was? In contrast, my own face was a refusal of that inheritance: blotchy, already showing signs of prepubescent acne and so much darker. I was furious that it wasn't good enough for her. Eventually I always gave in, curled up on the stairwell and allowed her to roughly rub the stick into my pockmarked skin.

There, that's so much better.

Two red welts, bruising both cheeks.

Now you look beautiful.

What I Hated Most of All

"Muni, you are just like your father."
Maybe she didn't really say that.
Maybe I only imagined it.

The Phone Call

Before my introductory call with the head of the station, I did what any good journalist would do: a little googling.

Turns out Don had worked at almost every radio station I'd ever listened to growing up. Online I found a lot of old photographs of him posing beside big-time rock stars like the Rolling Stones, Cream, BTO. He looked like a remnant from the 1970s himself in those shots: long bushy sideburns, big Coke-bottle glasses. In more current shots, he looked about sixty, maybe seventy if I wasn't being generous. Shorter hair.

"Is that Michelle?" a gruff voice said on the other end of the line.

"Um, yes . . . I mean no." *Get it together, Mahtani.* "It's actually, um, Minelle," I said, clearing my throat, trying to muster up some confidence. All those years of teaching in front of countless undergraduates in large lecture halls, coming face to face with growling administrators at the university . . . and yet I still felt like a child.

"I heard your audition tape. It's good. Not great. But good," he said roughly, emphasizing the word *good*, underlining it with his tone. "Holds a little promise."

I had recorded it, uttered a quiet prayer – *Bismillah Hir Rahman Nir Rahim* – and fired it off to my mother for approval. She had said, again, breathlessly, "*Mashallah*, Muni – it is so good!"

I took this measly bit of praise from Don now and held it close.

"I'm glad to hear it!" We have a joke in my house that you can tell who

I'm talking to based solely on the tone of my voice, not on what I'm saying. Speaking to my friend Roshni? Large guffaws, exclamations and snorts ensue. On the phone with someone I dislike? Shortened, clipped sentences, all consonants. And here? I could tell I was at my sycophantic, syrupy best. "Does this . . . mean you want to hire me?" I'd gone too far, and Don let me know it with a scoff. "I wouldn't say that, yet. After all, what do you really know about radio?"

The truth was not much. Don knew that. Why was he asking this question?

"I don't have experience in radio, but I do know TV," I stammered.

"You may know TV, but TV is not radio. It's an entirely different medium. We'd have to work hard to get you up to speed. How are you on taking direction?"

My mother always told me I didn't take feedback well. Mostly from her, but really from anyone.

I answered with an airy lie: "Oh, I'm great at it."

"Remember this isn't an academic show," he said icily. "I saw your resumé. I know you're a professor. I get that you want to bring that pointy-headed stuff to the show, but this is still entertainment, okay?"

"Oh sure, Don. I get it."

Just get the job offer, Mahtani.

Smile for the camera, sweetheart.

The Chance

Days later, Don called me again. I'd gotten the job.

Before I could fully feel the rush of excitement and relief, there was a crucial caveat.

"I'll give you a chance, Minelle, but I need to tell you this: you are going to have to slow down how fast you speak, and learn to speak *clearly*. Even now you're talking too fast."

When I was nervous, I sped up my speech. Really, I should have known better. I'd been practising to perfect my voice my whole life.

Book on Head

I tottered on the top landing, my toes curled on the stairs of my childhood home. A heavy maroon *Webster's Dictionary* balanced precariously on my head. My hands were in prayer position behind my back, pointing skyward. I was ten years old.

I walked slowly up and down the hallway. "Prunes, prisms," I said.

My mother nodded. "Say it again," she said. "Again. Enunciate. Punctuate *prunes!*"

I walked back and forth, back and forth.

"This is good for you," she called out.

I continued until my tongue felt twisted and my back ached. Finally, when I couldn't stand it anymore, I casually shrugged the dictionary off my head. "I'm stopping now, Mom! I'm going to watch TV."

Did I really do that? No. Not unless I wanted a walloping.

Back and forth, again and again, praying my mother would finally smile, tell me I was doing it right.

Prunes, prisms.

That night, I said my prayers dutifully.

Dear Allah, please bless Mom, Dad, Ray, the cat, the dog and the fishes. Please bless everyone and every soul, and please forgive everyone and every soul's sins. If any soul has cancer, diseases, afflictions and handicaps, please let them not have cancer, diseases, afflictions and handicaps from this second on, for the rest of eternity.

While I prayed, I blinked seven times with one eye, then the other. Always seven. My own private ritual.

Then I prayed the most fervent prayer of all: *Please God, please make sure I don't let my mother down.*

Ameen.

Practice made perfect. By the time I was in grade six, I had no fear in front of large groups and entered a public speaking competition.

I stood in black patent-leather Mary Janes and a frilly navy polka-dotted dress at a podium in front of my entire school.

I said my lines. I paused for laughter at the funny bits — I had every beat down.

My mother stood at the back of the gymnasium, glowing with pride.

Winners

I decided to turn to my friend Ing for advice. If anyone could help me figure out how to prepare for the radio show, it would be her. She'd been working in radio for more than a decade.

I'd met Ing during our TV producing days. Our friendship had been built on a foundation of loving juicy gossip, terrible television and shoe-shopping. We also spoke a lot about race and inequality, but that came a short second to TV. There was no one else I would have preferred to share the indignities of my day-to-day with. You probably have one of those people in your life, if you're lucky. I hope you do.

Ing also taught me a lot about disability issues over the years as she was a woman of colour, a disability advocate and a person with a disability. She was acerbic, but she always had a soft spot for me. I never understood why, though I was grateful for it. She always told me the truth, too — even when it hurt. And this was one time I really needed that.

I called her as I rambled through Winners on Granville Street, searching for a first-day outfit for work. I walked round and round the store for an hour as we spoke, fingering various fabrics, absent-mindedly trying on a cashmere cardigan, a scarf here and there. While I did so, my leg was quietly throbbing, moving from numbness to shooting pain to numbness again.

"Look, Minelle, I actually think this sort of job plays to your strengths. In fact, I'd argue it's letting you do what you already do as a professor but on a bigger platform: discussing race as it relates to the zeitgeist and what's happening in the wider world. But you have no background in radio. This isn't going to be easy."

I sighed, putting down a Ralph Lauren button-down shirt. *Too formal and conservative for radio.*

"I know, I know. I'm nervous," I said.

But Ing cheered me on and reminded me that this was a new adventure. "Maybe you have to give this a shot."

I still had no idea how to write a script, how to read out time codes, or even how to segue from guest to guest. The truth of the matter was that even though I'd accepted the job, I wasn't sure I could do it. I'd already had my second act by going from TV to academia — I wasn't sure I had it in me to do it again. I'd learned how to fit into the academy, learned the rigid rules of the intellectual game and then how bend them, if only slightly. Radio was daunting in a whole new way. I didn't even know what shape I wanted the show to take.

"But Minelle," Ing was saying, "just think about what you love."

What did I love? *Tell me what you love,* the expression goes, *and I will tell you who you are.*

The ground, the sea, the air, the sky — I had always been fascinated by the intimate proximities that surrounded me, the way the soft soil felt under my feet, the way the air was perfumed by apple blossoms in our backyard, the sound of the sparrows near my bedroom window. My mind struggled to revive snippets of conversations, words upon words, and hovered instead around the locations where conversations had taken place. I didn't think in terms of time and history; the geographies were always what fascinated me. Honestly, I even loved the word *place*: the way it sounded like *palace*, a lavish and comfortable geography on which to land — it had a spatiality that spoke to me. I did not have the words to write through this until I was much older, but I realized even as a child that identity is intrinsically related to geography: that who you are and how you are perceived have a lot to do with where you are. Geography was land, blood, body, heart, life.

I was curious to know how other people of colour created a sense of place for themselves. I wanted to understand how this shaped their sense of belonging, intimacy and home.

This, I thought, was what I loved. Place and our relationship to it was something I wanted to speak to, about and around with guests on the show. I was a geography professor, after all. I was trained to do this.

"I think this could work," Ing said. "But only if you keep coming back to what geography means to you, and what it means to your guests."

I told Ing I also wanted the show to be unapologetically antiracist, anticolonial and defiantly and definitely feminist. I wanted to insist on amplifying voices rarely heard in mainstream media.

"Good luck with that," she said, laughing.

When we'd worked in TV news, we'd witnessed how flippantly decisions about representation were made. Rather than seeking out new guests from a range of backgrounds who could offer different perspectives, panellists were chosen from a Rolodex of experts and the usual people were brought on again and again. In those days, you would be proud of yourself if you found anyone, absolutely *anyone*, who wasn't an old white guy and managed to put them on air. That was considered a pat-on-the-back contribution to diversity.

I wanted the radio show to be different. There were new stories, I thought, that I hoped I could share. Stories that remained submerged. I wanted to prioritize the sacred stories of those who are often disrespected in media. I wanted to focus on the specificities, identities, world views and representations of the colonized. It was at this point that I remembered something my friend Candis had told me.

She is Tahltan. She explained that anticolonial storytelling involves acknowledging "all my relations." It is a prayer of oneness and harmony with all forms of life: other people, animals, insects, trees and plants, and even rocks, rivers, mountains and valleys. Acknowledging all my relations is an inherent acknowledgement of place. It means gesturing to those ancestors before us, and after us; and it is a way to recognize the geographies of the past, present and future. This was something I hoped to do with the show.

But I also knew that in the colonial order of things, anticolonial stories are always threatening.

"I'm rooting for you, Minelle, but you know what you're up against too." Ing was right. I could almost hear Don in my head: *Stop being such a pointy-headed academic.*

I went home empty-handed from Winners but with much to think about.

Later, at home, I scrawled these words on a scrap of paper: *mobility, intimacy, movement.* I yearned to make them the framework for the program.

And this show name came to me: *Sense of Place.*

In dreaming about what the show could be, I was becoming hopeful. But still, I called my mother again and told her I wasn't sure what I was doing.

"*Junam*, be patient with yourself," she said, laughing. "You are so hard on yourself."

Translations

Maybe this would be a good time to tell you what *junam* means.

My mom used to call me this all the time. I always assumed it was a religious-tinged term of endearment. But the other day I looked it up for you. Here it is:

> *Junam* is another extremely common term of endearment, and perhaps a little more fun to say, because even the act of saying it causes your lips to pucker as if getting prepared for a kiss. *Joon* is the word for life or soul. Because Persians are prone to drama and exaggeration, this term is also used quite liberally. It can also be translated as meaning something along the lines of "my dear," but more literally you are saying "my soul" (Leyla Shams, *Chai and Conversation*).

Reading this stopped me in my tracks. I hadn't known it meant something this beautiful.

And then I found this description from *Oxford Languages*:

> **junam (noun): nosedive**
> steep downward plunge, esp. of an aeroplane

The idea of taking a plunge into the unknown — into loving something with such blatant disregard for yourself that you're willing to put yourself in danger for that love: *junam*.

Patience

As soon as I was hired, I started to design the show. I began to gather a constellation of potential key columnists, as we called them, to offer support, including a brilliant Tahltan lawyer (Candis's sister, actually), a renowned Canadian rock star from the band Chilliwack, a friend and criminologist I'd met during my undergraduate years and an acclaimed Asian Studies professor. They had far reaches into their own communities, so I hoped they would help secure guests and that the trust between them would create a more intimate space for conversation — that it might broaden the host-guest binary from two to three and create a different kind of conversation.

I wanted the show to be made for and *with* Black, Indigenous and other people of colour (BIPOC). To make it a priority to book their stories. These people would be artists, activists, authors. My quiet way to build a new nest of community in the place where I felt unmoored.

I turned to Toni Morrison for inspiration. She wrote that her work was "an effort to avert the critical gaze from the racial object to the racial subject; from the described and imagined to the describers and imaginers; from the serving to the served." I was not there to provide a voice for the voiceless. This assumes there is a *they* who don't have a voice and that you do. It assumes individuals do not have agency, and it positions you as a liberator of voices. That is not your — or my — job.

Arundhati Roy reminds us "there is really no such thing as the 'voiceless.' There are only the deliberately silenced, or the preferably unheard." (I just said that last line out loud three times, so you can hear it too.)

I was elated, terrified, thrilled — finally feeling like I was accomplishing what as a scholar I always hoped to do: bridge theory with practice. To make a difference in two worlds.

And in between all of this, I noticed something else —

My hands were no longer shaking.

Better

Two months after my visit to the ER, it was finally time for my appointment at the MS clinic. This time, I had Bruce by my side. I couldn't explain it, but I told the specialist my symptoms had been milder, fading. He asked me to follow his finger with my gaze.

At the end of the appointment, he said, "Your tests came back fine. We will keep monitoring, but you seem . . . better."

Better. What constituted better, now?

I called my mother and told her the good news. She squealed and said she had to get off the phone right that second. Right. That. Second.

"Mom, why?" I had more to say. I wanted to tell her about my plans for the show. My growing yet still unsteady confidence in my ideas.

"I have to go, Muni. I have to hit the mat."

Which, as you might know, means *I have to go thank God and pray.*

Travelling to India without My Father

I was in Mumbai visiting my father's family with my mom. My brother, Ray, was not with us. Neither was my father. I was about ten.

I thought there was an icy crispness to my aunt's voice when she spoke to my mom. A curt coldness. I couldn't put my finger on it. But I could feel it.

I called my father. I said, "Dad, Dad. Come here. Something is not right." But he demurred, said he could not come.

I hung up.

I asked my mom why my dad's family seemed to be bullying her. She said I was imagining things. But I thought I could see on her face that I wasn't.

Whispers, twitters. Doors slammed shut. Clipped phrases in Hindi. My Iranian mother caught every word.

I imagined what my aunts and cousins were saying about me. *Not fully Indian. Not Indian enough. Ugly.* Were they making fun of me? Her? Both of us?

I counted the weeks, days, hours until we could return home.

I began to believe that even though my mother spoke Hindi, Urdu and Bengali perfectly and felt more at home in India than in any other place in the world, after having spent much of her childhood in Kolkata, she would never be fully accepted by my dad's family. Was the colour of her skin, her religion, a curse to them? Her kind words, her thoughtful gestures all meaningless — no matter the tone of her voice, the sweetness of her smile?

Porridge with Blueberries

I got word that the station was ready for us to all go in and take a look around. The antenna wasn't up yet — that would take a while still. *Good*, I thought. I felt nowhere near ready for the show to go on air, though I had begun to tentatively line up guests.

As I took the bus to Roundhouse, I chewed on my nails. I knew I had the scaffolding of *Sense of Place* down. But that day, I had to finally face it: I had to sit in front of the mic and speak.

I took a deep breath as I opened the heavy glass doors to the station. Everything sparkled. It was all shark silver and gleaming. The station was replete with new technology, nothing like the machines I'd edited on at CBC. The lobby was decorated with gorgeous dark maroon leather couches and leafy plants that dotted the sun-dappled space. A change from my dark oak-lined lecture halls at the downtown university campus. There was even a bar up front with high-topped chairs and a fancy Italian cappuccino machine (which would be removed, tragically and far too soon, when it was found to be too expensive to continue to rent).

A pretty, freckled blonde watched me walk in. *This has got to be Tracey, the program director*, I thought.

"Minelle! Welcome!" she said, her face lighting up. "I'm so glad you're here!" Her warmth caught me off guard. She had that gift of disarming people with her friendliness. I recognized it because I liked to think I have the same superpower.

"Let me introduce you to Don." She ushered me over to a desk behind her. There sat a man with a shock of white hair. He stood up abruptly. Turned out he was shorter than I'd expected but as stern as I'd thought.

"Minelle?" Don said, furrowing his brow.

Uh-oh, I thought. *This guy really doesn't like me.*

"Nice to meet you, Don!" I said.

He was still looking at me as if he was trying to place me. "Glad you're here," he said gruffly.

I straightened up a bit. "I think I can do some good things here, Don," I said in a voice I hadn't heard come out of me in a long time. "I'm excited about it."

Don harrumphed, and Tracey grabbed my arm. "Let me show you around the station," she said. She ushered me through the sound stations used for recording and the backroom with a huge oak table. Then she introduced me to Aaron.

Meeting Aaron would be the very best thing to happen to me that day.

Aaron was tall. Very tall. Slim and trim. Crewcut. A friendly smile. I confessed to him I'd never done any radio, and he just nodded thoughtfully and said, "It's okay. I'll walk you through it." Aaron was a board operator, apparently.

"Um, Aaron?" I asked. "What's a board?"

He tried to disguise his shock with a cough and said, "Um, you know, where we control everything? The board with all the switches?" It was at this point he must have realized he was dealing with a neophyte — but, in what I would learn was his characteristic generosity, he let it go, the way he would let all sorts of mistakes I made go when I started the show.

I sat down at the desk where I'd do the interviews. In a stroke of genius, they'd found a circle — a legitimate round table — for us to sit around with guests. It was befitting of the station's slogan — *Our City, Your Voice* — and of the type of space I was hoping to build.

Aaron placed me behind a monitor and gestured to headphones on the desk. "Put those on, okay?" he said from behind the glass, where he sat by what I now knew was the board. "I'll speak to you through those."

I put the headphones on and craned toward the mic. I tried an awkward "Hello? Hello?"

"Let's do a sound test, Minelle," I heard Aaron say through the headphones.

What's a sound test? I wondered. And then *Good Lord! Is he going to ask me to speak off-the-cuff?*

But Aaron once again let me off the hook. He said, "Minelle, tell me what you had for breakfast this morning."

"I . . . well . . . I had oatmeal. Actually, porridge with blueberries and maple syrup. And I had coffee, and . . ." I continued on, going into detail about the bowl the oats were in, and the kind of coffee I drank (macadamia-nut flavoured, my favourite), as Aaron fiddled with the board.

Later, I understood what he'd offered me then: the generosity of being put at ease. Something I would try to bring to guests too.

Bougainvillea

The stories that really matter to me now are the ones I hardly registered back then. There are too many of those to count – and I can't hear them again. But in trying to cobble her story together, maybe I can tell you this one. This is the one told to me, the one I was gifted. I know there are different versions others might tell. There are always many others. Every story, always another story.

My mother's family was torn apart by World War II, but not in the ways you might think. My mother was visiting her grandparents in Kolkata – her grandfather was stationed there for work – when World War II broke out. She was three years old and travelling without her parents. Because of the war, it was at impossible to send little Farideh back to Abadan, and so she was kept in India with her grandparents.

I imagine her being away from her mother and what that must have meant for her. I sometimes wonder if this is why she later became a teacher – to give back to others what she'd once most needed. When her own mother was finally able to fetch her, she chose to keep her daughter in Kolkata and move the rest of the family there too.

They lived in a house framed in fuchsia bougainvillea. For years, I tried to imagine what this flower looked like, this blossom so foreign to me and yet so close to my mother's soul-home. Whenever she mentioned this flower, a dreamy smile would slowly appear on her face. It was only when I went with her to India at the age of sixteen that I saw what she'd seen daily for years: her childhood home still covered in the striking pink blossoms, bursting with brightness, that shocking splash of lush colour. The remnants of a home she loved, the only ones left.

"I brought you here so you could see my home, Muni," my Iranian mother said.

What impact did that have on my mother, growing up in an environment so different from her mother's geography? How quickly did her Farsi falter? How soon did she find herself stuttering through what I thought was her mother tongue?

When I heard her speak Farsi, I would see how she started, stuttered, hesitated. She would chide herself under her breath. But it wasn't her fault. In contrast, when she spoke Hindi and Bengali, another side of her personality appeared: joyful, animated, alive — her childhood come into colour, like bougainvillea growing on the vine.

Meet and Greet at Roundhouse

Having not found anything of merit at Winners during my talk with Ing, I donned a flowery dress, a flowing chiffon number dotted with purple blossoms I had brought from Toronto. The dress swirled around my thighs playfully. It was the first time the hosts would meet each other at the station.

When I got to the studio, I stopped in front of the door and grasped the handle nervously: tapping it one, two, three . . . exactly seven times, as I always did.

At the front bar, near the fancy cappuccino machine, sat the new hosts. Kirk was there, my friend who had recommended me for the job in the first place, looking smooth in a neatly pressed shirt. He gave me a sly smile. I hadn't been sure who else had been hired, but I recognized their faces right away. An old-school icon in music journalism looked almost exactly the way I remembered him from his days on MuchMusic. He'd become even better looking with age, as some men tend to do — women, of course, are never offered that same hollow luxury. His smile sparkled, and I felt star-struck.

All of a sudden, my floral dress seemed overdone and showy in the sea of black leather and weathered white T-shirts.

There was a freckled man with tousled red hair in a simple golf shirt. He smiled at me. My gut told me he was kind. Tracey came in, vivacious and enthusiastic, making introductions, asking each of us to share a few words about ourselves.

"I'm Kerry Marshall," said the man with the ginger hair, his booming voice bouncing off the walls. *Ah, now I get it*, I thought to myself. *That voice holds magic.*

"I've been the morning anchor at . . ." He reeled off a list of stations, a long list of acronyms that meant nothing to this Toronto-born radio listener. "I'm here to do the news every morning."

I knew then that I'd be working with him daily, and I felt nervous about interacting with such a pro. "Prepare, Mahtani, prepare," I said under my breath.

A guy who looked to be his thirties offered a smile. "I'm Cory Price, and I'm doing the music show at noon, *Live from Railtown.*" He shared which bands he was going to have on — a mix of famous Canadian stars and a few indie bands I recognized. He had a gentle ease about him. I liked him already.

When it came to my turn to speak, all the skills I'd worked so hard to master in the ivory tower seemed to disappear. I muttered something about how I'd be doing the mid-morning show, and the old-school icon boomed out, "Can you speak up?"

I looked up, startled, and tried to speak again — stuttered. I deliberately said very little about my life as a professor; I'd learned far too well how that gets read in media circles: *Oh you think you're the big expert, don't you?* I could see that most of the hosts were not paying attention to me — they'd already checked out, were busy glancing at their phones.

We were all ushered into the gleaming studio. My new colleagues settled in at the round table as if they'd sat behind mics their entire lives. I felt awkward, looked awkward. I shifted uncomfortably in my chair. I coughed, cleared my throat and stared at the mic, wondering how I was going to speak into it, daily, without anxiety.

Audre Lorde, in "A Litany for Survival," wrote:

And when we speak we are afraid
our words will not be heard
nor welcomed
but when we are silent
we are still afraid

So it is better to speak
remembering
we were never meant to survive.

Once upon a Time

Once upon a time, there was a man. He was Indian. He met a woman. She was not Indian. They overcame strife! Prejudice! Discrimination! And fell in love.

Once upon a time, there was a Brown man. He married a not-Brown woman. They lived happily ever after. Until they didn't.

Once upon a time, there was a Hindu man. He married a Muslim woman. This, of course, didn't happen. That is an oxymoronic nightmare. This cannot exist. The end. Scratch this paragraph.

Once upon a time, there was a mixed marriage. It didn't work out. Of course not. They never do. Right?

Once upon a time, there was a damsel in distress. She was mysterious, magnetic, captivating. Exotic. (Cue the famous theorist Edward Said here.) A man was entranced. He married her.

Once upon a time, there was a girl. She was the mixed product of all of these stories.

These are some of the ways I tell my origin story. After all, people love a fairy tale. Every story, always another story.

Mic Sock

During those early days trying to make radio, I discovered many gadgets unfamiliar to me. One of these things was a sock.

Do you know what that is?

I didn't either. Turns out a sock is a soft cylindrical cover that goes over the mic.

The sock sat forlornly on the table. It looked lonely. It reminded me of me.

Aaron told me I punctuated my *p*'s too much — I'm too punchy — and that I needed to soften how I spoke. He told me to put the sock on the mic. This would make my speech more palatable, he said.

Soften my speech. Make it more palatable. This made me laugh. I was being asked to tone things down. Be less loud. Now I would have help from this inanimate object, this thing that would muffle my voice.

I placed the sock over the mic and tried again. *Prunes, prisms,* I thought.

"Better, better," Aaron said.

I've always hated my mouth. By this I mean I not only hated what I said with my lips, teeth and tongue, and the macabre dance that entailed, but also what my crooked mouth looked like when I said it.

My mouth is marked, you see.

When I was three, I fell on a glass coffee table and tore my top lip open, blood spilling on the carpet. Ever since then, I've had a tiny crescent moon scar right above my Cupid's bow. I love having a reason to write those words, *Cupid's bow*, for you.

As I interviewed guests in those early days, a circumlocutory mess of anxiety and messy mispronunciations, I couldn't stop thinking about my ugly mouth: all its lousy imperfections, its inability to speak straight. I was haunted by a singular memory from my time in television years earlier. A well-liked news video editor and I were working furiously to deadline late at night in an edit suite. Edit suites are dark and cozy. If you've worked in one, you might know that they can breed a particular kind of unearned intimacy. The editor I was working with was hip and cool. He made me nervous. At one point, I let my guard down and giggled at a shot. He looked at me with distaste and said, "You look so funny when you laugh."

You look so funny.

Ever since then, I'd covered my mouth when I chuckled. I thought I could spare people the sight of my smile.

Ten years later, a reporter would write an article about mixed race identity for *Toronto Life* magazine and ask me for my official perspective as an expert in the field. We met at a coffee shop on the University of Toronto campus. When I read the published piece, this is what it said:

> Mahtani has long, dark hair, a toothy smile and a collection of features that are impossible to place on a map. When she was growing up in Thornhill, people would guess at her background without ever hitting on the actual mix, Iranian and Indian. "As a kid, I was one of the few minorities in my neighbourhood, and there was pressure to acclimatize to whiteness," she says.

You might be tempted to drill down on what I said there. About the pressure to be seen as more white. Maybe that's interesting to you. Maybe you wish I would tell you that I saw my limp little body as proof of the promise of mending. I promise I will say more about this later. Or maybe I won't. But for now, I want to ask you to focus on this instead: that bit where he said I had a toothy grin. This wounded me to the point that I called up the reporter and told him that what I looked like wasn't the story. The story should have been what I'd said.

After a day of gruelling interviews at Roundhouse I felt hadn't gone well, I would go home to cuddle my son, grapple with what to make for dinner and, later in the evening, grimace at the bags under my eyes and, most of all, stare at my mouth in the mirror.

That girl has her mother's mouth, I remember hearing a relative say once, disparagingly.

It's a good thing she has her father's eyes.

Good Fortune

Unfurled, it looked like a cartographic chart: a navigator's map to travel the salty oceans, from the Pacific to the Atlantic and back again. It was horoscopic, rife with details about my future.

Inside the cramped apartment in Mumbai, it was sweltering. Outside the rusty barred windows, the thin bamboo trees swayed gently in the scant breeze. The heat and humidity of the city were almost insufferable. My aunt was supervising dinner preparations in the tight galley kitchen. I savoured the scent of cinnamon and cardamom hanging in the air. *Puris* lay in wait in silver thalis, sweating under metal lids. My mouth watered.

The sounds of the city wafted in. Cars honking, dogs barking. I heard the punctuated laughter of store owners, their guttural accents so like my father's, voices I rarely heard on the streets of Toronto at that time.

The astrologer sat cross-legged on the worn Persian carpet, poring over the parchment paper, pointing out pertinent details to my parents. All Mahtani girls get their horoscope told at age nine. As my parents and the astrologer murmured quietly, heads bent toward one another, I looked out the window, hoping my brother, Ray, and I could go out later to play with some of the stray dogs.

The astrologer said something I couldn't quite decipher.

"Well, of course she has a great destiny. Look at her name! Her name is Minelle. It means *wish come true* in Arabic. *Man-al,*" my dad said, enunciating both syllables. "Wish come true!"

I could see what was about to happen next. My dad was about to launch into the story. The story he loved to tell. I steeled myself.

"You see," my dad said, flopping back into a puckered rattan chair, "we wanted our child to have a name that marked her as different but that also gestured to our desire for integration in our beautiful new country called Canada."

My mom grimaced, rolled her eyes at me. We'd heard this story so many times it was seared into our memories, word for word.

"We considered many names, but nothing felt quite right. Then mere minutes after this little one came into the world, an Arabic-speaking friend visited us in the hospital. She said, 'Why don't you call her Manal? It means *wish come true* in Arabic!'"

My mom sighed and tapped her long tapered fingernails on the hardwood floor.

"But it wasn't enough to call her Manal! We knew Canadians would struggle with it. So we decided to gesture to Canada's grand French Canadian culture. You know the name Michelle? You know it?"

The astrologer was picking at the frayed edges of the parchment paper. He'd checked out ages ago. He raised his gaze slowly to my father's, his eyelids stone-heavy. "No, sir. Tell me," he said in a monotone. *Can I get paid now? Bloody foreigners*, I imagined him thinking. My dad may have been Indian, born and raised, but he was now a so-called Westerner, coming back for an "authentic Indian experience."

My dad was not dissuaded by the man's apparent lack of interest. He was not telling the story for the astrologer.

"It's almost like a French name!" my father said, gesturing flamboyantly with his arms, knocking down a vase in the process. "You know, like the Beatles' song!" He started to croon off-key. "Well, we decided to make her name sound more French Canadian, so we spelled it like Michelle!"

The astrologer's expression didn't shift.

"*Are, baba* — you understand? So that the *goras* would get it! Treat her well! So she could fit in!"

The astrologer seemed to realize he had to say something. "Can we continue now, sir?"

My dad nodded vigorously. "Yes, yes. Tell us."

I knew what the astrologer was about to say held great importance for me. My cousins had been told that they would attend Harvard and Wellesley College. Years later, they would do just that.

The fortune teller made his declaration: "She is going to go to this school — Harvard. And . . . she will become prime minister of Canada someday."

Harvard? Prime minister? How could I live up to those expectations? I couldn't even master my multiplication tables. I'd only come in *second* at the science fair.

But I promised myself then and there that I would try to do anything to please my parents, to make them proud of me. I would go to Harvard — whatever it took.

My dad leaped up and did a little dance on the hardwood floor. "*Baap re!*" he said jubilantly. "I knew it! I knew it!" He took my hand, pulled me up, did a jig. I awkwardly tried to follow his lead.

My mom looked at us both, lips pursed, shaking her head. *You two*, I knew she was thinking.

Always you two.

The Rumpled Comforter

My brother, Ray, called me from Toronto, where he was living with our mother. He said that sometimes, late at night, he would pass her open bedroom door, glance in on her. He would first see her curled under the sheets. And then he would hear her quietly crying. When he gingerly inquired about the tears one morning, she admitted that she missed me. But she said nothing more, refused to delve into detail.

I imagine she'd expected to have her grandchild and daughter around for her retirement years. I knew she'd relished the thought of spending more time with us. But I had whisked us away to Vancouver, and there was a chasm of time facing her, a space of not knowing. Busy as I was at the radio station and with Cole, she and I still spoke on the phone daily, exchanged spirited texts with many exclamation marks, lots of emojis.

She never said any of this to me.

Attempts on Air

I'd been on the air for a few weeks, and I was finding radio to be surprisingly lonely work. The other hosts seemed to keep a cool distance from me. My polite, pleasant overtures to meet for drinks were cast aside, but always with courtesy.

I saw that I was not very good at this job. I talked too much or not enough. I never knew if my questions would hit the mark or resonate with the guests. I tried to create private moments in the studio with them, but my attempts to build a secret sanctuary often fell flat.

My favourite guests on the show were the writers on tour, publicizing their books. But some of them appeared otherworldly – and distracted. Part of it was my lack of experience, to be sure. But it was more than that. Only about half of the person I was interviewing showed up sometimes, if at all. Reading a memoir, you only get to know the writer of the story. Not the writer. The two are not the same. On air, I met some ephemeral version of the guest, the person they wanted me to see. They saved their best words for the page, not the microphone. Toni Morrison said she would play to interviewers' fixed ideas of who she was, or rather "disappear—shift into automatic and let them have any shadow to play with, hoping my smoke will distract them into believing I am still there. Because an interview is not an important thing." I didn't blame her. When authors spoke to me, their words were meticulous, economical. Meted out. They auditioned their lines for their true debut on the page, coming soon to a bookstore near you. Each radio interview was a kind of rehearsal for their next project — or the denouement after the real show of writing the book was over, part of an onerous and exhausting promotional tour.

But maybe this wasn't completely true.

Some authors' voices, if you listened hard enough, carried hushed secrets under their wings. I tried to eavesdrop on the things they did not say.

It wasn't my first experience with this, of course.

I remember huddling on the floor outside my parents' bedroom when I was four, listening to my dad's impatient voice, growing louder and louder. I was wearing a thin cotton nightgown with a mouse on the front of it. I was shivering. My mother's muted tones came through the closed door, her attempts to quieten him, her voice rising slightly and then falling. "Kish, please, try to calm down, darling."

Then snatched, rough words emerging from my father's mouth: "He said I was too *Oriental* to get the promotion. Really, can you believe it? *Maadarachod, chutiya sala.*" He spit out a few more splintered expletives in Hindi.

My mother tried to comfort him with more lilting words, some in Hindi, some in English. I couldn't make out what she said specifically. But I could hear the shape of the sounds.

Over the years, I heard enough to know that voices carry all sorts of secrets and histories. All the angry histories so present, pulsating in my father's voice, lulled inadequately by my mother's. And within the intricate interlacing of those voices was the hushed story of oppression.

I heard enough to know there is not just the story carried within the voice but the voice carrying the story.

I tried to listen for this in my interviews — to the words being said, to the stories not told beneath them.

Spring Music Festival

When I saw her wringing her hands, I knew it meant only one thing. Things were bad. When the fire-red tulips bloomed, and the kids at her Montessori school carelessly discarded their winter jackets to play outside, it signalled that her annual music festival was just around the corner. We knew what that meant. She would have to make some sort of public declaration in front of all the parents, welcoming them to the event.

"Save the date," she would say to my brother and me many months ahead of time. "You have to be there." This was non-negotiable, I knew. Even if I were in some far-flung country, I would be expected to come home to attend. In stark contrast to me, who never wanted anyone I knew to be in the audience for public lectures, who never wanted my parents at soccer games, recitals.

As a child, I used to find my mother's notebooks scattered around the house, pages scribbled with her meticulously crafted welcome speech. She would rehearse draft after draft. "Welcome, parents, to the Montessori North School music festival!" She always sounded a bit off-kilter, stilted, during her practice runs.

She would stand at our fireplace, a makeshift dais, reciting to me. "Punctuate *parents*," I would instruct. She was focused, driven, determined to get it right. I would catch her whispering her speech at the dining room table to herself, reciting it under her breath as we drove up to the school on the day of the event, thinking no one was listening.

I felt strangely maternal, watching her up on stage every year. I wanted to protect her from judgment. But it was strangely appealing too. I saw that her students' parents found her presentations endearing. There was no pretending that this was easy for her — no pretensions here. And that only made her more lovable.

Pebbles in Pockets

For every two interviews that seemed to go well, one went awry. It was also penetratingly lonely work. You were always working in a vacuum alone — I never knew if my questions would hit the right mark, or if listeners would connect with what was shared in the intimate, private moments between me and the guests sitting across from me. I could never really know. I walked out of the studio every day spent. All I had heard wasn't confined to the studio; it was shared in the sound waves. But it was all that was unsaid that I kept weighted down in my pockets, along with the crumpled pages of my scripts.

The Butter Knife

I was sitting in the cafeteria at the Canadian Broadcasting Corporation's national headquarters in Toronto. I was twenty-four, and I'd just started a new job as an editorial assistant for *The National*, one of the biggest news shows in Canada. I'd worked hard to get there, and I'd temporarily abandoned my PhD program to take on this job, so I was damned if I wasn't going to learn everything I could about TV producing.

I was sitting with the other EAs, all of them accomplished, bright and shiny young people with journalism degrees and experience at the best papers, the best magazines. I was eating macaroni and cheese and chatting away when one of the women at the table suddenly said, "You don't belong here."

I looked around, wondering who she was talking to.

"You don't deserve this job," she said, meeting my eye. "You don't deserve to be in the newsroom."

I didn't know what to say.

She picked up her butter knife and pointed it at my face. "You only got this job because you're not white. Plain and simple."

Everyone at the table seemed to be staring at something on the horizon only they could see.

"But . . . I'm working on a PhD. I've published in the *Toronto Star*. I know I don't have your credentials, maybe, but . . ."

"You don't deserve to be here."

No one said a word.

I left the table slowly, counting down the number of steps it took me to leave the cafeteria, to get into the elevator: *twenty, nineteen, eighteen . . . only a few more to go*. I hoped I would land on seven when I got to the elevator. I prayed I would.

Maybe my PhD didn't mean anything. Maybe I really didn't belong there.

James Baldwin said, "It's not the world that was my oppressor, because what the world does to you, if the world does it to you long enough and effectively enough, you begin to do to yourself."

I began to believe it myself.

I was a failure.

The Dummy Reel

"You free for lunch today?" Don said.

I could tell this was not just a friendly offer to grab a bite to eat. He wanted to tell me something, and he wanted to do it over food.

I said, "Sure," without much confidence.

On the way to the restaurant, he told me, "Minelle, I may have to cancel your show."

I was surprised — it was still so early. We'd been on the air for just two months; we didn't even have numbers yet.

At the Water St. Café, one of the fanciest restaurants in Gastown, Don speared a crab cake. These crab cakes were fourteen bucks a pop. Just for an appetizer! There was no way I could afford this place, but after the bomb he just dropped, I knew Don would pick up the tab. Making me pay for my own paltry soup would be too cruel.

After placing the morsel in his mouth, he delivered the details. "Minelle, you sound too dry and dull. You're not performing enough."

I stifled a gasp. *But I've been working so hard.* I took a sip of soup. It was salty and lukewarm. "But, Don," I tried to keep my voice level, "I've been listening to what the consultant told me. I'm pronouncing clearly. I'm not speaking as fast as I used to."

Don shook his head. "That's only part of the problem. You just don't sound like a radio host. In fact, it's so bad that one of the technicians took all the *um*s and *ah*s you've said on air and put together a dummy reel. It's been making the rounds in the newsroom."

My heart stopped. *People are making fun of me?* I'd suspected people didn't like me, but this was too much.

I knew I echoed people's body language when they sat across from me in the studio. I'd learned a long time ago that this kind of mirroring helps build intimacy, and I had selfishly adopted it. My mother liked to tell this story at dinner parties: a teacher was speaking to her, and apparently I was nearby. I was five. "Shh," the teacher said. "Little pitchers have big ears." From then on, I was considered to be an eavesdropper, someone who was always listening in, paying attention to details no one else would ever catch. It comes with the territory of being mixed race, I later thought to myself. Of always watching, learning, picking up clues to learn about the other side, the other way of being. Mirroring the opposite. But I'd been leaning into this too much. Lately, I'd been mirroring guests' voices too. When a guest said something animated, I'd been interjecting with "That's great!" or "Wow!" My interjections did not make for great radio. I could only imagine what that reel sounded like. Shame filled me. I put down my spoon; my appetite had vanished.

Don took another bite of his lunch. People had been laughing at the reel, he said. "It's hilarious."

I tried not to look shocked. It wasn't until later that I became angry and mustered up enough courage to tell the technician who'd made the reel to fuck off right to his face. With Don, though, I just sat quietly.

"You sound too much like a sex kitten," Don went on. "This isn't the Playboy channel or late-night radio. You have to put more spark in your step."

I felt humiliated. I thought I sounded professional with a smooth, clean voice. Isn't that what they wanted from me? I'd been trying so hard.

PART TWO

SOUND

"In radio, you have two tools. Sound and silence."

— IRA GLASS, in an interview with *The New York Times Magazine*

Humility

I knew I had to get better on the show. But I didn't know how.

Every morning, I would leave the house at seven, my little boy still curled up under the covers. I would take the 4 bus into Railtown from Kitsilano, set up shop in the corner of the JJ Bean café on Railway Street and start to prep. I scanned books for those moments of reveal that spoke to me. The moments that might resonate with listeners who tuned in to the show. I scoured previous interviews, looking for clues, trying to sleuth out what irritated my guests, searching for that special something that might make our conversation sing.

Reading so much in preparation for interviews with authors changed me. I read about two books a week. This made me want to write well, write better. My scripts changed with every memoir and novel I devoured. It's not that I replicated the authors' styles necessarily, but I continued to mirror aspects of their cadences and tones.

I made a wish list of authors I longed to speak to: Ann Patchett, Tom Rachman, Dani Shapiro, Margo Jefferson, Colson Whitehead, Gordon Korman (a beloved author from my childhood), David Chariandy, Lawrence Hill. My producers sometimes glanced at the list and, brows askew, asked, *Why? Why this person? They're not on tour right now.*

I know, I would say. *I know.*

I recognized the outrageous gift in being able to reach out to any author I chose. The show gave me a venue to develop a connection with authors whose work mattered to me. In this, I felt utterly selfish. But I didn't dare refuse the opportunity. Would you?

I began to feel for authors on an endless parade of interviews. As I listened to interview after interview, tinny headphones perched on my head in that coffee shop, I heard a needless cycle of pointless questions. Maybe hearing the inevitable awful question makes you cringe sometimes too. The bad questions fall into camps. What is it that Tolstoy said about happy families and unhappy families? I discover there are also endless ways of asking a bad question. They can be sycophantic: "I loved your book so much! How did you write such a good book?" Or sanctimonious: "Did you feel a lot of pressure to write a book as good as your last one?"

I, too, fell prey to these kinds of lazy questions.

I started to leave work berating myself, mumbling under my breath, "You're such an idiot," after particularly bad interviews.

I wasn't alone in recognizing my mistakes. Through the glass partition, I saw my producers wince during interviews. Their expressions often mirrored what I felt. My stomach dropped after I asked an impertinent or unanswerable question. Or when I threw in too much academic talk: an unneeded reference to Foucault here, a gesture to bell hooks there, trying to sound too smart for my own good. I even uttered once, with a childish, nervous giggle, "Edward Said would have a field day with what you just said!" This was met with blank stares, silence, a cocked brow.

I began to see that my ego was getting in the way. But I didn't know what to do.

It was then that I dimly remembered the time my mom forced me to write an essay on humility when I was seven. Behaving particularly impertinently and belligerently one day, I was ordered up to my room. My mom watched me storm up the stairs, her forceful footsteps following right behind mine. She firmly sat me down on my Laura Ashley duvet, the one dotted with tiny red tulips, and handed me three items: a pen, a piece of three-holed lined paper and that same dreaded *Webster's Dictionary* I wore on my head years ago, now serving an even more nefarious purpose.

"Write me an essay on the definition of humility," she said, eyes blazing. "Because it's clear you have no idea what that word means."

She stormed off, leaving me perplexed. I had no idea where to start. I thought maybe humility had something to do with humiliation.

Humiliation — now that was something I could work with. It was an emotion with which I was achingly familiar. I felt humiliated every day at school. My dark skin, the downy hair on my upper lip marked me as unattractive, different.

I turned the doorknob to my room, peered out into the hallway. My mother was sitting on her bed, and I could see her from where I stood. I tentatively tiptoed towards her, and asked a question. "Mom? Is *humility* the same thing as *humiliation*?"

"*Beti*, no," she said gently. "Not at all. They are not the same. You have no modesty, no sense of what it means to be humble, *junam*. You are becoming even more arrogant, egotistical, apathetic. You will look up the word *humility*, Muni. And you will write me a two-page essay. And you will explain to me why we must all learn the value of humility. You, most of all."

I stormed back into my room, slammed the door. But I wrote the essay.

Years later, when my mom was profiled in the *Markham Economist & Sun* for her countless acts of generosity in the community, she refused our compliments, told us not to buy so many copies of the paper. "No, no. It's nothing. It's nothing. Let's talk about something else," she said. "Anyway, it's haram to brag, Muni."

How does one translate the experience of humiliation into the act of humility? The relationship between these two words has always spoken to me. What does it mean to be modest, to demonstrate humility, when one is constantly humiliated as a person of colour? What does it mean when the experience of anything that even resembles immodesty, for even a moment, already seems so rare and fleeting?

That essay my mom made me write stuck with me. It made me think long and hard about what it meant to conduct an interview with humility. How to take myself out of the equation, to make space for the interviewee. It made me more conscious of how I needed to make space for them to speak with greater honesty. The power I wielded had nothing to do with the power of my voice.

An old Arabic proverb goes something like this: "Open your mouth only if what you are going to say is more beautiful than silence."

And another Arab proverb: "The mouth should have three gate-keepers: Is it true? Is it kind? Is it necessary?" I tried to govern what I said through this trio of questions.

If it wasn't true, kind and necessary, I kept my mouth shut.

The Car Game

How did you learn how to ask questions?

This is how I think I learned — from my mom.

As soon as she pulled out of the parking lot of Toronto Montessori Schools, where she was a teacher and I was a student, she would encourage me to start.

"Come on, Muni."

"Darling, how was your day?" I would begin. At this time of day, the car would be suffused with late afternoon light. I think it was 1975, which would have made me four.

"Oh, thank you for asking, Mama!" she would sing out. "It was a hard day. My teacher didn't really listen to me when I made suggestions . . . and the lunches didn't come on time."

"That's too bad, that's too bad, Mama . . . I mean Farideh. What did you do?"

"Oh, Mama, I didn't know what to do! But then Sara found the lunches and then we . . ."

"What happened next, Fari?"

This world existed all the way from York Mills to Finch, past the subdivisions, past the manicured lawns of the suburbs, until we reached Centre Street in Richmond Hill.

As soon as we careened into our driveway, she would turn her head around to me, smile and say, "Thank you, Muni." She would be back.

And I could then say, "Thank you, Mama." And we would go back to business as usual, my small hand in hers, as she unbuckled me out of my car seat.

Did this really happen?

I'm not sure.

My mom told me this story.

I don't know why she told me that she used to do this with me. Maybe she wanted me to know she was rarely asked questions the way she asked them of me. Maybe it was fulfilling something for her that she never received as a child. I don't know what makes me more weepy: knowing that she felt this way, or knowing that she confessed this story to me.

The Iran-Persia Debate

When I was seventeen, my father and I scoured countless American university brochures featuring carefree undergraduates frolicking on impeccably manicured campuses; they were the very embodiment of a bright future to me. But although there were many brochures, there was only one that really mattered – only one I slept with under my pillow. We had, of course, decided that I was going to Harvard. Only Harvard. It was the school for me. Remember the words of the astrologer?

My dad had applied to Harvard Business School a year earlier. I still remember his crumpled face when he received his rejection letter.

We looked for clues as to how to excel on the SAT and ace the interview portion of the entrance examination. I was granted an interview, as all applicants were, and the interview was to take place in Rosedale, an affluent part of Toronto.

We drove all the way from Markham on that cold and frosty November Saturday morning. I was wearing my best dress – sedate but not boring – and tiny gold earrings from India. If you are Indian, you know just the kind of gold I am talking about here: twenty-four karat, more orange than yellow, with just a bit of sheen. My dad bought them for me years ago. I felt proud to be Indian in those earrings. I loved them.

I was feeling a bit cocky but a lot more nervous as I walked into the office of the Harvard alumnus who would be interviewing me.

I wasn't sure what he did for a living, but I was sure it must have been a good job because good Lord, look at that furniture! The sofas were inviting in their burnished chocolate leather glory. You know the look of a well-worn leather sofa? They were tufted with gold studs. And the rugs, the rugs all looked . . . well, like the rugs in our home. Masterfully embroidered hand-hooked rugs from Iran, I guessed, with intricate images of Iranian men on horses and gardens. The rugs made me feel at home in that incongruous geography.

I plunked down on the sofa, and it made a sudden *whoosh* sound. The interviewer wore what I assumed was a very expensive jacket. He opened up the folder with all my details, nodding at my accomplishments: an article in the *Toronto Star*, president of the Welcoming Club, Soccer Club, cross-country, band and on and on.

Then he said, "I see that you're Persian!"

"Excuse me, sir?" I said, wobbly.

"You know — you're half Persian! That must be wonderful, to have access to that extraordinary culture."

I shook my head slowly.

He ruffled through the paperwork again, clearly surprised. "But it says here that you're from Iran?"

"Yes, yes — my mother is from Iran. That's true," I said. "She's from Abadan originally, and then she moved to Kolkata, then to London and Toronto."

The man frowned, looking at me like I was the stupidest person alive. "Miss Mahtani, you do realize that Persia and Iran are the *same place*?"

I was always, always told: never say you are from Persia. "You are not a rug, Minelle. You are a person. You are not an object. Persia — that is not our country. That's the word the British use to speak about my homeland," my mother would say. "It is not my country, Persia. Say Iran. Iran."

"They are?" I asked, responding to his question with a question.

And to be honest, I didn't know.

Persia and Iran — the same?

Years later I would learn that this statement was actually debatable. I joined the Iranian professional club at my university, and we discussed how we wanted to describe ourselves: as Iranians or as Persians? One of the Iranian studies professor insisted, with not a little authority, "Persian is more accurate. Iran is simply the country. Persian is the culture." Others disagreed.

I felt shame in the Harvard interviewer's office that day. I knew I had given the wrong answer, and I never told him why I'd answered the way I had.

Or did I answer correctly?

I answered the way my mom would have wanted me to.

It came as no surprise when the rejection letter landed in our mailbox. Well, it was not a surprise to anyone except my father, who clung to the letter with such deep sadness. Once again, Harvard had broken his heart.

Breaking Dawn

As a teenager, I was always incredulous at how cheerful my mother was when I woke up, even when the gloom of a cold, dry Toronto winter morning permeated the house. Half-asleep, my brother and I would stumble down the stairs. Grumpy, rubbing the sleep out of our eyes, responding in monosyllables to her affectionate "Salaam, *junam*," as she placed steaming bowls of oatmeal in front of us.

We never said more than one or two words to her those mornings, the brightness of the ceiling lamp mixing wretchedly with the early dawn darkness. The shadows on her lined face would linger, her face alight with something resembling joy.

Before I went on the air, I'd think about Don's words and try to sound upbeat like my mother. I tried to channel the love that embroidered her voice on those deep-blue mornings. I began to laugh on air. First it was forced, then my efforts slowly become more natural. I tried to forget those piercing words I told you about from the video editor I admired at CBC. Please don't make me repeat them.

I also tried to discard my carefully crafted scripts. My producer threatened, jokingly, to take them away from me so I would ad lib more. But it was a struggle. I felt myself falling back into my old patterns of preparation. *Sound like yourself*, I kept telling myself.

But what does that mean — *sound like yourself*? I began to wonder: was it possible I was failing at my job because I'd been unwittingly trying to sound white? I had been mimicking the voices on NPR and CBC. Wasn't that was what I was supposed to do?

Briana Barner: "The standard public radio voice is objective, void of distinct cultural identity and discernable accent. It is white. As objectivity is favoured in journalism, our racialized voice can reveal our identity, our heritage, our background. It can connect us with the people where we're from. This is not often welcomed. The standard voice is a white voice."

I had forgotten that sound is always racialized and gendered. I had forgotten that whiteness is simultaneously unmarked. My content was intentionally non-white. But the medium through which I was producing those stories was not.

Cole Arthur Riley: "How much is the sound of your own voice worth?"

I'd been working so hard at sounding standard — at sounding white — that I sounded like nobody at all.

Breakup I

I had just finished high school and would start university in the fall. Not Harvard, of course, but McGill in Montreal. I possessed the kind of confident arrogance particular to naive youth who are about to blindly and blithely embark upon a new adventure.

My mother announced that she was taking me out to dinner. I wondered why. As soon as we sat down at the restaurant, she ordered a chilled glass of Pinot Grigio. In those days, before she became more religious, she drank occasionally at home but rarely when we were out — that's how I knew this was serious. Was something wrong? Had I disappointed her somehow? I braced myself.

"I'm leaving your father," she said.

I was struck silent.

She slowly explained that she has been waiting years, *years*, to leave and now that I was going away to school, she could go too. She had waited long enough.

I replayed moments from my childhood over and over again, wondering how I hadn't seen the signs. I remembered his nightly vodka and sodas as soon as he came home from work, ice cubes clinking loudly in his Swarovski crystal glasses, remembered Mom shushing Ray and me. *He's had a hard day. Please be quiet.*

She continued to cite the reasons she was leaving him, but I zoned out, unable to listen.

My dad, shell-shocked by her decision. He said he hadn't seen this coming. Wire hangers swung in my parents' formerly shared closet, sadly singing their miserable lullaby of loneliness. They missed her beautiful colourful dresses, striped silk shirts, scarves, saris, *salwar kameez*. Her Tea Rose perfume was conspicuously missing from the bare dresser.

The house seemed quiet without my mother and brother. They'd found an apartment a few streets away. I continued to live with my dad. There were reasons why I didn't go with my mom and Ray. My dad couldn't be left alone, I told myself. He was devastated. He had no one else.

I turned down McGill. I decided to stay close to home and attend the University of Toronto Scarborough instead. I was gutted, but with the divorce pending, money would be tight, I knew. And anyway, I hadn't gotten into Harvard, so what did it matter where I went? Every other school was the same. I couldn't give my father Harvard, but at least I could give him my presence at home, to help him through this somehow.

My dad shared the separation agreement with me. It felt heavy — it was at least forty pages. I read it next to him in the Pontiac Ventura, for some reason.

"Dad," I said, incredulously. "This is completely unfair. You're giving away everything! You can't do this!" He sat in the driver's seat, mute. "You can't sign this, Dad!"

I didn't speak to my mother for a few years after that — not really. When I saw her, on weekends and on some weeknights here and there, I was standoffish. I chose to quietly seethe. I blamed her. I did not yet see that the way he treated me was the opposite of the way he treated her. He revered me and placed in me all his dashed dreams. He showered her with disdain and spoke to her in a patronizing tone, when he deigned speak to her at all. I had read the silence between them as agreeableness. But it was the opposite — it festered with regret, resentment and years lost. Regrets tend to breed hostile resentment. I didn't see the slights, the years of quiet, because I was subsumed in his adoration of me. I couldn't possibly admit it to myself.

Years later, an astrologist would say to me that I was like a deity to my father; in a previous life, I was the goddess to whom he prayed.

The Sweetness of Doughnuts

Shortly before my mom was diagnosed with tongue cancer, shortly before her speech became slurred, she sent us a children's book. This was not unusual. She was constantly sending us gifts. But this book — it was different from any children's book I'd ever seen before.

It was called *That's What Grandmas Do! A Wish for My Grandchild.* The cover featured a bunny, ostensibly a grandma, with her grand-bunny, in pastel colours. It was a press-and-play recordable storybook that, according to the cover, allowed you to "read to loved ones even when you can't be there . . . [using] Voice Save™ Technology."

The first line of the book is "If every wish I make with love could magically come true, I'd gladly spend them all on you. That's what grandmas do!" I pressed the first button. My mother's voice warbled out, clear and true, as she read out the line.

Cole and I read on, then reached this part: "I wish you pancakes shaped like hearts in great big gooey piles . . . plus yummy doughnuts cut in half to look like happy smiles!" My mom, with her sly sense of humour, added her own *ameh-biance* to it. (*Ameh* — a noun — is *aunt* in Farsi. My first cousin on my mom's side came up with an alterna-tive meaning for it: *Ameh* — a verb — "to add beauty, exquisite joy, aes-thetic pleasure to a task, an object, a moment." Creating *ameh-biance.*) My mother read the line and then ad libbed, making reference to my vegetarian, health-conscious partner: "Cole, I don't think your dad will be very happy to hear this, you eating all sorts of gooey sugary things . . . I'm just joking!"

I could hear her smiling between the words.

I started trying to smile when I was reading my show intros.

John Stuart Mill

I kept thinking about how to bring more of myself to interviews. When the best interviewers spoke, you could hear their personalities shining through. I wanted to do the same. I longed to speak with fewer empty interjections, so I started to rely more on facial expressions to encourage the guest across from me to go on. Letting the silence speak for me. Trying to find ways to coax the shy little birds out from under writers' tongues.

Erica Heilman: "A good interview is about love. It's about finding and falling into the humanity of another person, so that listeners can fall in too."

The morning that Adam Gopnik, writer for the *New Yorker* and memoirist, was on the show, I had thought with a pinch of vanity about what I would wear to the interview. I had been scrounging around in my closet for something appropriate. I'd amassed a large collection of sheath dresses, bought on sale at Judith & Charles, the upscale boutique around the corner from us in whiter-than-white Kitsilano. But none of them seemed right. I hastily picked out a stained white linen shirt and my distressed J Brand denim. Maybe dishevelled, but at least I looked slightly fashionable.

I thought about Don's latest missive to me: "You have to post more to social media — it's the only way to get your numbers up." I *hated* posting on social media. I always fretted over what to post, who would read it and what would be said about it. But I heeded

Don's words, knowing he was probably right. Without overthinking it too much, I posted this on Twitter: "What does one wear to an interview with Adam Gopnik? My guess is your best linen shirt." (It was my only linen shirt, but who was going to know?)

I felt cautiously ready for the interview. I had done my usual: I had read all his books and then some, looking for clues to his passions and aspirations between the lines. But it was my partner who ultimately helped me figure out my approach.

When I walked into the studio that day, I saw Gopnik was already there, sitting on our vintage (read: threadbare) sofa. He was sporting a crisp violet-grape linen shirt. I smiled at the serendipity. Then he looked at me with his trademark grin and said, "I saw your tweet about your shirt. I decided I'd follow your lead and do the same."

It was then I realized I might have more leverage than I'd thought — they say imitation is the highest form of flattery. Perhaps I could take some leaps of faith in the interview.

As I'd scanned several of Gopnik's memoirs at home the night before, poring over them with my yellow highlighter, I'd asked Bruce what he thought about Gopnik. My partner is an avid *New Yorker* reader, and I suspected he had some thoughts about the columnist. Bruce was at the sink, washing dishes from dinner. (He knew better than to have me wash them; I am a hopeless domestic, which he's known from the start of our relationship.) With a stained dishtowel slung over his shoulder, soapy sponge in hand, he turned to me and said, "I'd like to know more about why he's obsessed with John Stuart Mill."

I put down my pen and smiled at my partner. I knew why Bruce wanted to learn more about Gopnik's interest in Mill. It was because he shares the same obsession. My partner completed his PhD on Mill. Bruce's interest in Mill stems from his own intellectual commitment to understand modern liberal democracy. But Gopnik's interest in the thinker, about whom he'd written copiously, remained veiled.

Bruce put away a chipped dish in the cabinet and shrugged. Walking over to the bookcase, he pulled down a book. "You may want to take a look at this."

It was the book that Bruce had written on John Stuart Mill.

Bruce then explained to me that Mill had experienced a troubled childhood. I revisited several of Gopnik's memoirs and wondered if there were similarities there. But I wasn't sure I was comfortable asking Gopnik about that; the line between personal and professional can be easily blurred when speaking to memoirists, and it's easy to ask impertinent questions. I didn't want to do that. Was it worth the risk to go there in a twenty-four-minute interview?

But when Gopnik walked in wearing a shirt inspired by mine, and yet so different (more beautiful, more pressed, more clean and perfect), I decided to take the chance. He could shut me down, but it was worth a try. Our interview began, and I asked him the questions that a radio listener might expect me to ask.

But then I said, "You've just offered me a great segue, thinking about liberty and freedom. I think it's very hard to think about those things without thinking about John Stuart Mill — a theorist I know has deeply influenced you. I have to admit, my interest in Mill stems from a personal place, because my partner is a big John Stuart Mill scholar. So it's hard for me not to think about this book you've written about marriage, without thinking about both my partner and Mill."

Gopnik looked at me expectantly, almost as if he was asking, *You know where you're going with this, right?*

I continued. "I wanted to ask if we could talk about the similarities between you and Mill in some ways. Maybe I'm wrong on this. I want to just have some fun with you like you do with Mill in some of your works. You, like Mill, are also a bit of a prodigy. I mean, you graduated high school at fourteen. But Mill, on the other hand — he suffered a bit of a mental crisis at that tender age, and some suspect that it inspired his sympathy for the oppressed. Are there lessons for us around Mill's crisis of faith and the ways you speak about mourning and loss in this book about marriage?"

Gopnik waited for the real question.

I took a deep breath and asked what I really wanted to ask, which was "Did you ever go through anything similar to what Mill had gone through?"

Now I waited. I roamed his face. He was trembling, his eyes wide open. Then he looked at me with a bit of wonder.

"I did. I did. I think anybody who sort of has that experience of earlier precocity inevitably has the experience of an adolescent breakdown. I had mine maybe not as grandly though. I have never publicly talked about it as a meltdown. But there was a period of time, when I was about fourteen, until when I graduated from high school, where I never felt just about right. And it happened through nobody's fault. And up until the age of eighteen when I was completely out of school, not really doing anything, when I was just sort of totally on my own doing nothing but reading in a library and just listening to music . . . and I developed passions then that have served me well since. I don't think about it as wasted time in that way — it's when I discovered Rodgers and Hart and P.G. Wodehouse and Proust and so on . . . But yes, I think I can say [I had] that absolutely same experience of feeling cracked in some way."

After we finished the interview, Gopnik smiled and said, "How could you make that connection? I've not spoken to anyone about that time in my life. No one has made that link. How could you know?"

For the first time since I started the job, I felt triumphant.

Breakup II

The evening before I left Blake, the white boy with whom I had bought a house, with whom I had spent six years of my thirties, I met up with my friend Jean who was visiting Toronto from Vancouver. We shared a sweating carafe of Sauvignon Blanc on a patio in the Beaches and chatted easily about what we were going to do the next day: we were going to speak on a panel about mixed race identities. We shared notes about how we planned to approach the panel and discussed how we would try to explain to the audience the differences between mixed race from an Indigenous perspective and from a racialized settler perspective. I came away from our meeting elated, as I always did after time with Jean. I admired her a great deal; plus, she gave the world's best hugs.

Despite it being only early summer, I found the heat stifling. As I walked home, the sun setting over the horizon of Lake Ontario, I noticed a young woman tottering down the street near my house, her eyes crimson red. She was wearing peeling black patent stilettos and fraying cut-off jean shorts. Then she was screaming, her words indecipherable. She flailed in the middle of the road, cars swerving around her on the busy street.

I ran home, breathless, and found Blake. Shaking, I told him to come out, this woman needed help. Never one to leave a damsel in distress, he followed and gently approached the woman as he would a hurt animal. She hollered at him, told him to keep away. He tried everything, cajoling her, but she refused to move to the sidewalk. She almost got hit by a passing car. I saw that nothing my boyfriend was doing was helping. He called the police.

The sound of the sirens seemed to echo in the heat. The cops demanded the woman get out of the road. She refused. They dragged her into the cop car, handcuffed her, told her to stop resisting. She continued to resist. They began to drive away, but somehow she was able to open the door, and she toppled out of the car as it was moving. I muffled a gasp, my hand to my mouth. The police stopped the car and stuffed her back into it. She was screaming as the car squealed away from our driveway.

Nothing to see here. Go home.

That night, Blake and I had another blowout. I had put on my best smoky-blue, fine-lace teddy in the hopes I could convince Blake to have unprotected sex with me. He rejected me again, told me he just couldn't see himself having children with me because I wouldn't be a good enough mother. That I was too messy, and that I probably wouldn't, he reminded me again, take his kids to the museum. This was the fight we had over and over again: that I called the Royal Ontario Museum the Royal Appropriation Museum. I thought of the ROM as an ostentatious, colonial white fortress teeming with stolen objects; he had an annual membership.

I started to argue, again argue, and then I thought suddenly about the woman screaming on the street. I took off the teddy I was wearing, folded it neatly, placed it in our perfectly designed closet that Blake had built himself and went to sleep.

The next day, I woke early. I briskly and efficiently packed two Loblaws plastic bags with three outfits. One was for the TV panel later that day — a BCBG Max Azria grey pantsuit. The second was for the gala dinner I was attending that evening for the Canadian Ethnic Media Association — a chiffon number, egg-yolk yellow and light and pretty and new. The third was a set of old polka-dot flannel pyjamas from Joe Fresh. I placed two bracelets on my wrists that I knew Blake thought were rather gauche, but I loved them.

As I walked out the door, Blake gave me a peck on the cheek. "See you later tonight," he said.

I shook my head. "No. I'm not coming back."

He stared at me, his face ashen. He wanted an explanation. I said I no longer had anything left to give him, and I walked out the door.

Jean made sharp, excellent points on the panel that morning. I felt pretty good about my performance too. Years later, I rewatched the recording from that day and noticed a clarity in my eyes, a sureness to my voice. The bracelets adorning my wrists.

After the panel, Jean drove me to a friend's house, my bags of clothes at my feet. We couldn't stop grinning.

Later that night, at the gala, I sat in the gardens of Casa Loma, surrounded by lush greenery, barely blooming butter-coloured tulips tinged with cardinal red. The smell of early summer and hope were in the air. My friend Brenda sat next to me in a beautiful peacock-blue dress. I told her what had happened, and she smiled, said it was about time. I spent the next two weeks with friends, moving from home to home, from couch to couch. I wasn't unhappy. In fact, I felt free, unfettered, for the first time in years.

It really was about time, I thought.

Just Sayin'

Just when I thought I was getting better at the job, Don marched up to my desk and gruffly announced, "I want you to do a story on genital mutilation — it's getting a lot of press and we should be covering it too."

My body stiffened. "Don, I really don't want to do that story." I tried to explain that the subject of female genital mutilation is almost always covered in a way that favours Western points of view, rather than capturing the issue's complexity. I wasn't sure I could do it justice. I knew I couldn't. I shook my head no. I was not going to do it.

But he wouldn't have it.

He kept asking why, and I kept saying no. He wasn't used to people saying no to him. He was the boss. Finally, his face suffused with anger, he said, "I just don't get it. Just find someone and put them on air and talk about it!" Normally when he was upset with me, he would send me a terse note that ended with "just sayin'." But that day he wasn't just sayin' it in an email. He was telling me strongly — in person.

With a small burst of confidence, I stood up and said, "No. Is this your show or mine?"

I could see that he thought it was his station. Which it was, I guess.

"It's your station, Don, but it's my show."

"That may be true, but you do have to listen to what I am saying." And that is when the truth tumbled from his mouth — all the concerns he'd had about me, carefully preserved over months, all the critiques he'd heard from others — all in one go. "Minelle, you know what? Bottom line is you are not producing interesting radio. You're producing radio that feels like . . . well, homework. It doesn't have an entertaining feel. Your program has no vision, and others feel similarly." He continued, breaking out into a long litany of complaints from his friends and, apparently, other seasoned radio hosts who coveted my job. "It's boring, your guests don't know how to do radio, it's difficult to listen to, you're not really covering all aspects of the city . . . You know we had a radio consultant from the States listen to your reel? We sent it to him and you know what he said? He said you were stilted, scripted and not spontaneous!"

My first reaction was admiration — what astonishing alliteration. Then I remembered he was talking about me, and none of those adjectives was complimentary.

I heard my mom's voice in my head: *prunes, prisms*. I sat up straighter. "I disagree with you, Don, and if you don't like it, you can fire me!" Where did that come from? I wondered.

"Fine! You better get representation!" Don said and stormed off.

Swear to Frog

When my father died, I was on a research trip in Vancouver. It was 2006. I was staying at the Sylvia Hotel, that beautiful old-fashioned hotel by English Bay. I'd always wanted to stay there. I was on the hotel patio with two colleagues, discussing our research project, when I realized I had forgotten my pen. I said I had to rush up to my room for just a minute. When I reached my room, I checked my phone, which I'd left by the bed. I had ten missed calls from my brother.

Why would my brother be calling me so urgently?

I panicked. I have always rushed to the worst-case scenario. My aunt used to call me "doom and gloom."

Hands shaking, I called him back. "Ray? What's wrong?"

Silence.

"Ray, tell me. What's happening?"

"Minelle," he said. "I have terrible news."

Heart pounding, I started to get hysterical. "What is it, Ray? Tell me! Just tell me!" I didn't want to know and yet I had to know. I felt nauseous.

"Dad's dead."

The two words a life, a death, a thread, a beginning and an end.

"No, no . . ." My voice cracked. "That can't be true! Say *swear to God*! Say *swear to God*!"

My brother teased me our entire childhood. He'd make up silly things to try to fool me all the time: "Minelle, I bought this three-hundred-dollar jacket for only ten bucks!" or "You know that album you hate? It went platinum in two days!" Things like that. I'd look at him wide-eyed and say, "No way! That can't be right! Say *swear to God!*" And he'd laugh in my face, smirking, saying slowly, drawing it out just to really torture me. "Swear to . . . frog!" And that's how I knew he was joking. That it was all just a big joke. Surely this must be a joke too.

"Say *swear to God!*" I screamed again. *Please say swear to frog, please say swear to frog . . .*

"Swear to God, Minelle. Swear to God."

That's when my world turned upside down.

My father, gone. This couldn't be happening, this couldn't be possible, how could it happen . . . all the doubts and fears I'd had my entire life coming to fruition.

Ray told me Dad had been found in his bed after a massive coronary. His shih tzu bouncing up and down by his side, wondering why she wasn't going out for her daily constitutional. The building concierge, noticing that he hadn't seen my dad in some time, was the one who discovered him. He called my mother, who came with my brother to find his lifeless body in the apartment.

It poured that day in Toronto, apparently. A weeping sky, befitting the death of a great man, I thought. The whole world should grieve.

I remember heading down the hotel elevator and stepping outside. In absolute disbelief, I looked at my two colleagues and said flatly, "I have to go. My dad died."

I remember them sitting on that sun-drenched patio in English Bay, not saying a word. Just looking at me — and then the condolences, empty words I had said countless times to others, now directed my way. "Oh, Minelle, I'm so sorry, I'm so sorry . . ."

I remember my dear friend Sylvia picking me up, taking me to the airport. She sat with me at YVR while I waited for my flight home.

I remember shovelling uneven pieces of Swiss Chalet chicken into my mouth, my favourite, now cardboard. Sylvia gazed at me with concern. She would fly out days later to offer me comfort as I moved through the next stages of the process: cremation, funeral, probate. All those previously empty words that would come to hold an entirely different freight for me.

I never made it back to my apartment. I went straight to my mother's house. When I saw her, there were no words needed. My parents had been divorced for years, but she was still close to him; they talked fairly regularly, not out of necessity but by choice.

That night, my mom, brother, and I held a private vigil of sorts. We collapsed on the sofas in her living room, our legs tucked under us, her cats swishing beside me, the newly arrived shih tzu curled up on Mom's lap. We talked about all the things he loved: Stan Getz; the *New York Times*, particularly the marriage announcements; Impressionist paintings. Gorgeous gabardine suits in muted shades of olive, mauve, taupe. The sound of children laughing as they played basketball in the park just below his apartment on the Esplanade. And, oh, how he loved to cook! Elaborate Indian meals, recipes he had inherited from his father, a restaurateur, and his grandfather, a restaurateur before him. "Sindhi," my dad would say proudly, "we are Sindhis, Muni, never forget, we are entrepreneurs. It's in our blood." We talked about how he moved to London after having his dreams of being a pilot dashed because his eyesight wasn't 20/20; how he went into advertising and then eventually communications at the Ministry of Education. How his temper was legendary, only matched by his fierce generosity. How he could level you with the blink of an eye. How I was terrified of his wrath and at the same time adored him with an unparalleled ferocity.

Together, we reminisced with a lack of linearity.

We talked about him in the past tense for the first time. Several times I spoke about him in the present, and then with a sickening feeling I remembered, and I would return to the past tense, knocked back down into history.

What I remember most about that day is my mother. I remember her generosity in indulging us as we shared stories, despite the multitude of misinterpretations, the quiet cruelty inflicted on her by my father. How she shared memories with us, too, holding that space.

Still, in a circle we went, grasping for stories beyond our grief, until we felt sated, saturated in memories that held up our cracked hearts, if only briefly.

The thought, coming to me that night, head on pillow, with unabashed fear: *What happens when it's Mom's time?*

I hoped never to find out.

The Medical Report

Miraculously, Don didn't fire me. Once we both cooled down, we pretended our last exchange had never happened. But the resentment still simmered between us.

I kept trying to improve. I read my scripts out loud in front of the mirror. I tried to enunciate even more clearly and slowly. I sent recordings of the show to Ing and my friend Marichka who also worked in radio. They offered sage advice, advice that scorched my ego but that made me work better and harder. And as I slowly became more confident on air, the show received accolades: a community builder award, a photo spread in a flashy upscale magazine, a piece in the university publication *Academic Matters*. I received handwritten letters from famous authors on thick manila card stock, telling me how much they appreciated my unusual take on the interview process. I interviewed Lisa See, Gabor Maté, Lawrence Hill, Ann Patchett. The interviews were at times glorious, magical. We started getting fan mail. Don forwarded one letter to me:

> I'm writing this note to convey how dearly I cherish *Sense of Place*. It offers timely, thoughtful analysis and coverage of issues that cut to the heart of what affects us — belonging, creative expression, inclusion, inequality. I especially love your consistent, compassionate and expert hosting, Minelle.

When I share material from *Sense of Place* on my social media, EVERY TIME folks comment on your talent and charismatic presence. Your scriptwriting is as exceptional as your ad libbed and dynamic responses on air.

"Our numbers are up," Don said, scanning the reports. He was still furious with me, but because I was garnering some praise, we had reached a sort of quiet truce.

People were tuning in. Keep up the good work, I was told.

I couldn't hear the praise. I was unable to hear the praise.

It was around this time that my mother's tongue cancer was declared.

PART THREE

THE MOTHER VOICE
AS STRESS RELIEF

"The Latin root of the word *person* means 'to sound through,'
in turn implying a listener: We sound through to something
other than ourselves."

— MARIA POPOVA, The Marginalian

The Cold Sore

The long-distance call crackled.

"Salaam, *beti* . . ." she said in her perfect cadence. The reception was not good on my cellphone — I could barely hear her. "I went to see the doctor about a cold sore that isn't going away . . . I am sure it's nothing."

I tried to assure her, assure myself, listened to my own voice say over and over again, "I'm sure it's nothing, Mom. Don't worry. I'm sure it's nothing."

My great-grandmother died of tongue cancer. That knowledge hung pregnant in the air between us, unsaid. We mimicked each other's empty reassurances. But I wasn't convinced, and fear bubbled up in me.

My mother never worried about her health — actually, she rarely complained about anything. A yoga buff, non-smoker, non-drinker for years, she ate mindfully and encouraged others to do so as well. Every day she brought an extra helping of her steamed organic broccoli for her beloved students at her Montessori school, downed a putrid mixture of oregano oil and water at the first sign of a cold.

I was unnerved by her muted anxiety, struck by it, and tried not to think about it while I was on air. But how could I not think about it? I tried to be detached from my personal life at work, focused. But I still found myself sobbing uncontrollably in the staff bathroom those early days, counting the number of subway tiles on the walls, wiping away tears, hoping like hell that no one would catch me.

Google Tabs Open Just before Her Diagnosis

Judith & Charles sale! 20% off fall pieces
How to write a voice-over on the radio: tips for success
Recap of *The Affair*: Season 1
Dealing with an impertinent boss: when white supremacy
    rules your workplace
Blue Ruby Jewellery
Rob Brezsny horoscopes

Google Tabs Open Just after Her Diagnosis

Vitamix sale: 10% off if you act today!

Superfoods for dealing with cancer: the brilliance of Brazil nuts

Naturopathic treatments for cancer — Costa Rica retreat

How to avoid suffocation for patients with tongue cancer

Best head cancer specialists — Toronto

Turmeric — the magic drug

Losing a grandma: how to help your child deal with grief

Cheap last-minute flights to Toronto

Best Estate Lawyer — Markham

Rob Brezsny horoscopes

Questions I

I flew back to Toronto to help out my brother with our mother's medical appointments. We'd decided to split up her care. I would fly back as much as I could, and while there, I would care for her full-time. But I knew I couldn't stay in Toronto for too long. The radio show was daily, Monday to Friday, and Don bristled when I left for even a few days. It wasn't easy to find a fill-in.

On one visit to Toronto, I drove my mother to Sunnybrook's cancer clinic. Maybe you know it. I hope you don't. It's a massive cancer treatment centre on the outskirts of the city. We were in the waiting room. All around us were mothers, grandmothers, fathers, uncles, sons, some sporting knitted caps to warm up their balding heads, all of us waiting in ridiculously uncomfortable chairs. I heard a smattering of Farsi, Arabic, Mandarin. My mom, dressed up beautifully but looking so fragile.

We finally got in to see the oncologist.

I peppered him with questions using the techniques I had sharpened over months in front of the mic. I was careful to enunciate clearly, to not duplicate questions. *What is the prognosis? What surgery do you recommend? How long is the recovery period? What should she be eating? Will the Ensure provide her with enough nutrients . . . to keep her alive?*

There were never enough questions to ask him, and his answers were never enough. There was no answer that would explain the cancer away, no answer that would make me feel more settled, safe, that would make me feel able to breathe again.

I flew back to Vancouver, five hours away, and felt the sting of leaving my mom behind.

When I got back to Roundhouse, I found myself choking down sadness, unable to speak, tongue-tied, forlorn, furious and flushed by my lack of fluency. I checked my texts constantly, hoping to hear from my mom. When I didn't, I was immediately braced by the unflappable belief that she had choked, fallen, or that some other terrible thing had happened.

The terrible thing had already happened though.

In the studio, I cleared my throat and tried to ask questions of my guests that deserved to be answered. But what questions could I possibly ask, what questions would make my guests feel welcome, secure, able to speak?

I turned to philosopher Frantz Fanon, who reminds us, "O my body, make me always a man who questions!" But as in the hospital, my questions were never enough.

The limits of my questions. Judith Butler tells us that the question is "how to work the trap that one is inevitably in." I was trapped in silence, even as I tried to clear my rusty throat.

Philosophers Gilles Deleuze and Claire Parnet write, "The aim is not to answer questions, it's to get out, to get out of it."

I remember the famous interview-whisperer John Sawatsky telling me at the CBC, as I sat through class after class of professional development training, that the most important question we can ask in an interview is "What do you mean by that?"

What do you mean by that? Make the guest repeat themselves, over and over, until you get the answer you want. Until you get the perfect clip. Until you hear what you want to hear.

I used to think this was a brilliant question. Now, I'm not so sure.

What do you mean by that? The burden of extraction placed upon our interviewees — because, of course, they are seen as our interviewees, naturally, our property — with us forcing, dragging, pulling the information we so violently demand from them, wrenching it out from under their tongues, like bloodstained molars in their mouths, that process of extraction at the heart of colonial practice. We refuse to meet them on their own terms; instead we insist that they meet us on ours. We refuse the risks, dangers, opportunities of egalitarian intimacy.

What do you mean by that? I don't understand your story, we are saying. Tell it to me in a way that makes sense to me, that fits with my world view, my approach to seeing, feeling, talking, reading.

Welcome to Sense of Place. *I'm your host, Minelle Mahtani.* I said this over and over every morning, into the mic. Host? Host to whom? Was I really a host? If so, who were my guests and how could I acknowledge that they were gifting me with their stories, daily? I yearned to dissect the binary of host-guest, particularly given that some of us are but guests on stolen Indigenous territory. Pairs are often assumed to be a love story. Sometimes they can be violent, too.

I wondered how I could escape this trap I was inevitably caught in.

The coloniality of the interview, I scribbled in my journal at that time. It's a moral question, of course. To approach the possibility of an anticolonial rhythm and sound in journalism, a revolution in relationality — in the ways we relate to and connect with one another — is required, but what kind of revolution? I kept thinking about quiet revolutions. Not revolution as a spectacle, but as a moment in which everyone participates . . . whether they know it or not. That new social order — it's never spontaneous. It's not sudden. It's relational.

INTERVIEWER: "What are you angry about?"
BASQUIAT [smiling]: "I don't remember."

When I came across this exchange, I had to read it a few times in order to understand what was happening in that moment. The interviewer clearly assumed that Basquiat, a Black painter, was angry. And while I can't know if he really was angry or not, the assumption was startling to me.

Basquiat responded with what I see as humility and grace — explaining with a smile that he couldn't recall what he was angry about.

That anger — it is relational.

Maybe he was also saying: *It's not your business to assume I'm angry.*

I thought of the poet and novelist Anne Michaels, who said, "We forget the power of the small act of love. We forget how powerful that is. Often, we feel hopeless in the face of history, in the face of economics, in the face of these large forces, but really the small individual act can be incredibly powerful."

But what of that small individual act? How can one speak in that moment? Who decides the terms of engagement? I thought about how questions often gesture to a pre-existing point. Questions as cage.

We tell students to be curious about an answer, about a story. Ask questions! No question is too stupid, small. Ask away! But maybe we give too much credence to all questions, as if every question holds equal weight. We forget that questions can be cruel too. The ignorance laden in some questions. The agony of the question *where are you from*, of course, but there are others too. What guileless curiosity can do, unfortunately, is inflict unintended harm.

This is what I thought about then, and my worry about my mother was affecting my ability to work.

Bruce

When I broke up with Blake, I was hard on myself and thought staunchly, *When you fall in love next, try to find someone who is slightly less broken than you this time around.*

I was visiting Vancouver, my favourite city in the country, away from prying eyes and pressing commitments. It was August, and I was about to embark upon a month-long journey into hedonism, or so I told myself. I'd be damned if I wasn't going to eat, drink and sleep my way through this town. I was single and free. I wore a pretty white cotton dress. It was short-short with thin scalloped ribbons as straps. I am telling you this because I thought I looked cute.

My friend and I were walking near Kitsilano Beach when she suddenly glanced at her watch. She was late to meet another friend at a café, she told me. Did I want to tag along? She mentioned his name. It was familiar to me. I had skimmed his book a while back and had recommended it to a student. It was about whiteness and race, and though I had my doubts about a white man writing about race — always have, always will — I figured I'd come and meet the guy, even if just to judge the hell out of him.

My friend said she had to move her car, but that I could easily walk to the coffee shop from there. I don't remember why I didn't just go with her. I agreed blithely, without knowing exactly where I was. I'm only a *social* geographer, as the in-joke goes, and have no sense of direction. This was not my city yet, and despite its obvious grid plan, one a mere child could follow, I walked the wrong way. West, not east. North, not south. I started to run when I realized and I arrived late, of course, panting, sweat on my brow, hair out of place. I knew I couldn't possibly look pretty now.

They were sitting outside, sipping cappuccinos. When they saw me, my friend started to laugh. *What happened to you? It's so easy to get here!* Bruce didn't laugh at me though. He offered me a slow, sweet smile.

And I thought to myself, *Maybe he is slightly less broken than you.*

In an academic research paper, I once wrote, "An unusual pattern tends to emerge among women of mixed race when it comes to their dating practices. From 13–18, they tend to date white men. From 18–35, they search out solely partners of colour. But from 35 onwards, they often search out partners with whom they share something in common — a shared love of a particular kind of music, or hobby. Something beyond a racial similarity or dissimilarity, something beyond race, if that is ever possible."

What I remember from that time: us curled up on the couch in my sublet in the West End, me feeding him slices of Okanagan peaches at the height of the season, sweet slow kisses as the juice dribbled down our chins.

The Ground

My prayers took on a different shape when I found out my mother was sick.

I'd always had a nightly routine: I did *wazu*, the washing of my face, body, feet, hands; carefully put on a hijab; and rolled out my prayer mat. I went through the motions, bending down and kneeling to show my commitment to God. But after her diagnosis, as I uttered the words of my prayers out loud, the way my mother had taught me to say them, I noticed that there was electricity reverberating in my voice. A desperation, a need, a plaintive demand that everything had to be all right. A begging of sorts.

As I hit the ground, my forehead smacking the cold stone floor just so, I thought about how freighted down I felt. *Freight* — a word I use a lot. That, and *scaffolding* — the structures through which we construct our day-to-day. *Freight* feels so much more accurate, and poignant, than *weight*. Freight, for me, signals a heaviness that we as people of colour are all bound to carry, the endless demands placed upon us that we are forced to bear.

But what happened as I hit the ground to pray was that some of that freight was lifted from me and pulled to the ground.

What if I imagined that freight not as a chore, a burden, but rather as a way of being closer to the land? Not as anchor, but as connection to something greater than myself?

I started a small new ritual for myself. I made sure both of my feet were firmly planted, and I uttered a teaspoon of a prayer in my stilted Arabic: *Bismillah Hir Rahman Nir Rahim*. And in saying that, with my feet on the ground, I was saying to the land, *Take my story and please take this prayer.*

His First Words

My son, Cole, at eighteen months old. Perfect in every way, at least to me.

My mom was playing with him on the floor. She wouldn't get sick for another year. She looked at him thoughtfully and said, "He isn't speaking yet. Right?" I glanced up from where I was washing dishes. My sudsy hands started to wring. "No, not yet. Why?" Too late, I realized my tone said everything I was thinking.

"He should be speaking by now. I think you need to take him to the doctor. Something is wrong, *junam*."

I abruptly turned off the tap and said, "No, he's fine. Nothing to worry about."

She went back to playing with Cole. But first she drilled me with a look, a look that insisted I was wrong. I couldn't stand it when she thought she knew more about parenting than I did. Surely I knew my son better than she did. He was my child, after all. Not hers.

That night, I told Bruce about this conversation and hated myself for it. *I shouldn't even mention it; she's just acting up.* In the dark corners of my soul, though, I wondered if maybe, just maybe, my mother did know something I didn't.

Bruce could feel the anxiety rolling off me and reassured me that Cole was fine, that he'd talk when he was ready. But I couldn't shake the feeling that he was wrong, that I was wrong.

We made an appointment to see the pediatrician.

Cole sat on a white blanket of paper that crinkled underneath his tiny body. The doctor asked him a few questions, and Cole laughed, smiled.

The doctor smiled sympathetically in turn and said, "He may be slightly delayed. We can make an appointment with a speech therapist, if you want. Or we can just monitor it . . ."

I stopped listening right then. The alarm bells rang in my head: *shewasright-shewasright-shewasright*. I railed all the way home from the doctor's office, the subway train rattling us as I spiralled down. *This can't be happening*, I thought. *He has to be fine.* "This is it," I told Bruce. "He won't ever speak, ever. Something is wrong, my mom knew. She knew."

Bruce tolerated my rant, held Cole tight in the BabyBjörn. Cole was oblivious, delighted by the bright lights of the subway car.

When we told my mom what the doctor said, her face darkened. *I told you so*, she said without saying a word.

When Bruce took Cole into the daycare the next day, he sought out Zeb, our favourite daycare worker. Zeb had long dark hair, bright lively eyes and a wry sense of humour — a big throaty chuckle we both loved. When Bruce relayed what we heard from the doctor, she burst out laughing.

"Are you kidding me?" she barked. "There's no way that kid won't speak soon. He's just waiting, listening for the right moment. He's absolutely, completely fine. He is just waiting! You watch!" She laughed again, took Cole gingerly from Bruce and swung him around. "Isn't that right, Cole?" Cole gurgled, giggled with her.

Still, I fretted. I read up on developmental delays in toddlers. Apparently, boys tend to develop language skills later than girls, but in general, kids may be labelled "late-talking children" if they speak fewer than ten words by the age of eighteen to twenty months, or fewer than fifty words by twenty-one to thirty months. Cole still wasn't speaking at twenty months. Not yet.

A few months later, still no words. And then a barrage of them burst from his mouth, all at once, like gunfire. First, it was *Dada, Mama, cat, dog, DAT!*

Zeb grinned at us. Thwacked me playfully on the back of my head. "Told you you had nothing to worry about."

I smiled weakly. *Fine. You were right.*

When I told my mom triumphantly, "Cole is speaking!" at first she didn't believe me. She asked me to place the phone near him.

I could hear her saying to him through the line, "*Junam,* speak to your nana!"

Cole obediently responded back with "Nana! Cat!"

She was thrilled and said, "I am so proud of you, Cole! So proud!" When I returned to the line, she said nothing to me.

I said, "See? See?"

She scoffed. "I just wanted to be sure," she said.

Flash forward a few years: intricately designed tales emerge involving bright orange pumpkins and cherry-red Popsicles and UFOs and Beyblades and cheeping birds and big yellow buses and . . .

"Mama, can I tell you a story now?"

I find myself saying, again and again, "Yes, *junam.* Yes. I'm listening."

Shingles I

I was trying to get in the mood to finally make Cole a Halloween outfit — he wanted to be a ghost. At the same time, I was drafting a letter to the surgeon in Toronto, begging him to see my mother because the waiting list for the ear, nose and throat (ENT) expert was so long. But as I wrote, something kept itching under my left arm.

I kept scratching and scratching. I was convinced it was from the silk dress I was wearing that I'd recently taken to be dry cleaned. It must have been the solvent they used. But it continued to bug me all day, but I ignored it until I finally took off my dress and looked in the mirror. What I saw were scabs, welted scabs, dripping with blood, wrapped around my chest and under my arm like a tight scarlet ribbon.

I took a photo of the welts and sent it to my mother, along with a caption: "I wonder what this is?"

A second later: "Go see a doctor NOW."

But I ignored her. I decided that it must be nothing and made the choice to watch an episode of *The Good Wife* instead. It would go away, I reasoned. It couldn't be anything serious. It was only a rash.

The next day, the pain was excruciating. This couldn't be from dry cleaning solvent. I made an appointment to see a doctor, and when I took off my shirt, he clucked and said, "You should have come to see me sooner. Now the antiviral won't work."

He told me I had shingles.

I told him that was impossible — shingles is an old person's disease. He looked at me like I was an idiot and shook his head. "No, Minelle. It can also come on during periods of intense stress." He then reminded me that I wasn't as young as I thought I was. The luxury of not thinking about your body for months, years . . . the privilege of a healthy body. Now the stress was eating away at my body, delicately nibbling away at my peace of mind.

I learned the condition can linger for months, sometimes for years. The pain of knowing my mother was dying was making itself known on my body. My body was speaking loudly to me, saying, *She is going soon.* I'd refused to listen, and now my nervous system was acting out like a petulant child. I was furious with it, and because I was, it acted out even more. I came across the words of Elaine Scarry, who once said, "Physical pain has no voice, but when it at last finds a voice, it begins to tell a story." The bleeding blisters told a tale I was not yet ready to tell.

Psychics

When I met Bruce, it brought an almost abrupt end to my lifelong near-obsession with psychics. I'd consulted with them regularly before. But no more. My prayers had been answered in the form of this curly haired man.

But when my mom got sick, I started to go again. I needed answers. I needed them now.

I called my favourite psychic. She lived in Norway. Her assistant booked the appointment, charged my credit card 150 dollars for thirty minutes over the phone. The psychic's proclamation? "Oh, sweetheart. She will heal, but it will take time. Have her take feverfew, try thieves oil on her tongue . . ."

I took copious notes; I was so hungry for hope.

Another psychic, on a 1-800 phone line (I was that desperate) said, "They will cut it out in surgery."

She would be fine. Relief. They knew the answer.

My friend Mary Lynn told me at the time that horoscopes are a form of epistemology — that long word for a form of knowing. Is this why they call an astrological table an ephemeris? I hung on to this ephemeral knowledge as if my own life depended on it. Which, I guess, it did. I read somewhere else that astrology is merely self-love: a way to get to know yourself better. I scoured my horoscope daily, searching for clues that would allow her the chance to live. When they gave me a glimpse of possibility, I felt buoyant. When they didn't,

I was desolate. And so I would search for another horoscope until I found the answer I wanted.

Ah. There it is.

Superstition and science. Why was I convinced that they were at odds with one another? To deem them opposites is not to see the beauty that connects them, threads them together. I was no scientist, nor would I ever be. I mean, I failed physics in high school twice. I still count on my fingers. But Einstein also believed in the power of luck, chance, fate. But was that the same as superstition? Did I believe in horoscopes because I was superstitious? The mathematics of horoscopes . . . The actual chances that you will fall into one of those camps — Aries, Pisces, Scorpio — is one in twelve. And how often have I read another sign's horoscope and thought, *Good God, this is perfectly me*, only to discover I'm reading the wrong one? And how could I believe in luck when as a social scientist I knew luck could so easily be weaponized as an excuse for people to blissfully ignore systemic oppression, a neo-liberal way to pretend the trap we're caught in doesn't exist and is outside our control.

I remember reading somewhere that astrology could never be considered an objective way to answer questions. Astrologers can't be considered scientists, right? They don't use that old formula of *purpose — apparatus — method — observation — conclusion* that I diligently memorized in high school chemistry class to make sense of the natural world. Isn't that a key part of science? Critically evaluating whether explanations can be proven? And therein lies the violence of the opposition. They are not opposites: they feed off one another. Oppositional binaries. A scientist could hardly believe in the science of signs, right? And yet this other way of knowing became a kind of science to me. I believed in it with a reverberating fervour that guided me through my mother's illness.

Questions as wishes. Before Bruce, I had wished for things, so many times: a partner, love, a job. And I relied on mystical people to answer my questions for me: a tarot card reader, an astrologer. I placed hand-written prayers and wishes in the cracks of the rocks at the temples I visited in Osaka. I prayed to be engaged. And months later I was engaged, a ring on my finger, but to the wrong man — Blake.

I realize now I was asking the wrong questions. Instead of asking when I would find a partner, I should have asked why I was asking for one.

Are superstition and science the same as listening and speaking? Of course not, but science is always speaking, pronouncing, telling us what is right, declaring. One has to listen quietly to superstition. It doesn't always have a clear voice, a colonial voice that rings with formal logics as we have come to know them. *Shh.* It is under the whisper. Pulling you toward it. You have to be silent. And stay still, very still to hear it. Close to the ground. Down to the earth. Do you hear it now? Don't scare the little sparrows away.

Sometimes I hear it in the shape of a cumulus cloud, or maybe in the edges of my son's laughter. And other times I feel it so close that I could almost grab it, but it is always just out of my reach. I have to be paying close attention.

I've always trusted in another language to guide me — and maybe this is why I sometimes think I'm a terrible academic. I trusted, and still do trust, in the language of signs.

I looked for the feathers, the stones, the clouds shifting and changing: the signs that she would be okay. The superstition held within it a hope, a promise, but no guarantees.

Questions II

Around this time, I interviewed Michelle Jacques, chief curator at the Art Gallery of Greater Victoria. She had worked at the Art Gallery of Ontario for years before heading west to take the job. She is Black — but, of course, this is not her only story. She came to the studio directly from a long flight; she'd been in Milwaukee adjudicating an art show. I knew she was exhausted. I handed her a coffee, made small talk before we went into the studio. She smiled at me wanly. I adjusted the mic in front of her, cleared my throat. I wanted to ask her what it was like to be a Black chief curator in one of the whitest cities in Canada. About what it was like to trespass into those white spaces. The heaviness and burden of those opportunities, of those cages. But I knew that conversation was unlikely to be coaxed to the surface in our short time together. (And we know it is not safe to tell these stories; it is not safe to open one's mouth to tell these stories.)

The interview unfolded perfunctorily. Then I asked her, "You have had a long-time collaborative relationship with performance artist Anna Banana. You have said that her work appeals to you because hers is a practice that is primarily situated in her relationships and interactions with others. Might you say the same about your own practice as a curator?"

That moment. In that moment, she stopped. What I think I saw: a wry smile, her eyes dancing mischievously, recognition on her face. *Yes*, her look said. *I see you. I see you seeing me.* And that is when the interview suddenly and instantly shifted course. That moment of relationality: when I saw her on her terms, not my own.

Not much later, I was given the opportunity to interview Colson Whitehead as he was doing the rounds with his novel *Underground Railroad*. I had a list of thoughtfully curated questions in front of me, but I jettisoned most of them when I felt intuitively that they weren't going to fly. Instead, I asked him what constitutes a Black sense of place, quoting from the Black scholar Katherine McKittrick who has written extensively about Black matters being spatial matters.

"Why is space and place so significant to Black authors?" I asked.

Whitehead replied that he'd grown up in Brooklyn, which had an inextricable impact on his identity. "I remember when the World Trade Center came down, and I went to see my therapist, and I was like, 'I don't know. I thought they'd always be there.'"

His therapist said, "It sounds like you're describing your parents."

Whitehead told me he broke down at that moment. "It's definitely inextricably tied in my hometown and that story, I think, really gets at the heart of the matter in so many ways. You have these two looming figures on the skyline. You don't need to have a degree in psychology [to figure] that one out."

I've thought a lot about that moment since. I've wondered how that particular question led to him telling me about that moment with his therapist, one he later told me he hadn't spoken about in other interviews. I've thought a lot about his answer too. I've wondered how he made the decision to share that story, what ancestral energies passed into the studio to allow for me to be blessed with it. Reading McKittrick's powerful work provided a place for me to ask a question that Whitehead wanted to answer intimately. In making himself more seen, in taking that risk, he gave me a space to feel more seen too.

Hearing Whitehead speak about his parents moved me. It made me think more about my parents' broken marriage. What Whitehead's answer did for me was help me see how the binary that had shaped my thinking for years — Indian, Iranian — was an empty cliché. I became obsessed, instead, with the spaces between those words. What could I do to create different spaces for different stories, different sounds?

When I asked questions of guests, I realized I was making tiny wishes; dreaming that they could answer a question to which I longed for the answer. What is each question if not a wish? A wish to know more, maybe — but maybe more than that, too — to hear a point of connection. Am I hearing you? is the question I was really asking.

But maybe it was also a matter of trust — and who was, and wasn't, in the room that day. It's not something we talk about, but there's a certain intimacy that can exist between BIPOC — sometimes, not all the time — and that intimacy can flourish when white people aren't present. There can be a sense of ease and shared understanding.

My horoscope in Rob Brezsny's "Free Will Astrology" from this time told me what I needed to know. It moved me so much that I kept it, pasted it in my journal:

"If you don't ask the right question, every answer seems wrong," says singer-songwriter Ani DiFranco. I suspect you may have experienced a version of that predicament in recent weeks, Pisces. That's the bad news. The good news is that I expect you will finally formulate the right questions very soon. They will most likely be quite different from the wrong and irrelevant questions you've been posing. In fact, the best way to find the revelatory questions will be to renounce and dismiss all the questions you have been asking up until now.

I started to think about omission as presence in question-asking. How what is *not* there tells a story, a story about colonized processes of listening. How listening in itself can be a cage if you aren't paying attention to the sound of ancestral voices.

Now I know to look for what is not said in interviews. Science journalist Ed Yong says the crucial questions a doctor should ask a patient are "What have doctors gotten wrong in the past when treating you? What assumptions should I be careful not to make? What did they miss?" And I think this trio of questions allows for another story to be told: one that pays attention to the colonized histories of those silences.

Indigenous storytellers had much to teach me about questions, I began to see. Tanya Talaga, the renowned Ojibwe journalist, says that journalists are trained to ask who, what, where, when, why and how: "At the root of this approach are two questions that don't often make it into the news but should. They are: how do we want to live together and how might we find paths forward?" My time interviewing made me rethink the currency of the five Ws. Which of these Ws actually challenges colonial ways of thinking? My mind went to the work of scholar Patrick Wolfe, who said, "Settler colonizers come to stay: invasion is a structure not an event." This captures the idea that the settler colonial invasion of Indigenous lands was not a phenomenon of the past but is continually reproduced. And then I realized that thinking about colonialism as a structure, not an event, offered up a strong critique of journalism pedagogy. The Ws as taught in journalism school mostly address the who, what, where, when — less so the why. Journalists tend to focus on the event, rather than the reproduction of that event, or the *structure*. It is about the present spectacle, rather than the intricacies of the intersection between geography and time. They want to know the what, who, where and when but not always the how and the why, and how it happened before. There was a focus on the newness, rather than the reproduction of it all. A kind of violence occurred through the repetition of colonial question-asking.

My conversation with Whitehead opened up a space for me to ask new questions — not just to guests but to myself. Why wasn't

I asking myself the kinds of questions I was posing on the air? Didn't I have the courage? Or maybe I felt like I didn't deserve them. I wasn't delving into my own history the way I was delving into my guests' — reading over their words, scrutinizing their lives with care. I wasn't showing myself that same generosity of spirit.

I started tentatively by posing the question I hadn't dared ask myself.

What was I going to do without my mother?

Breastfeeding I

Another question for you: What does it feel like to not be able to feed your child?

I really hope you don't know.

I am unfortunately familiar with this experience because a day after my newborn son came home from the hospital, he wouldn't suckle at my breast.

We tried everything. Bruce watched on, helpless but without judgment. Forever the faithful journalist, I scoured countless websites, searching for tips that would trigger more milk, have Cole latch.

"It's *you* who has to latch," the lactation consultants told me.

But what does *latch* mean? Connect? Merge? Fuse? I wasn't sure. "Trigger the letdown," they said. To the uninitiated in the breastfeeding world (me), this statement was confusing. The letdown is the gushing down of milk one eagerly anticipates when feeding one's child. This did not happen to me.

I hated these words they used in relation to my body, this body of mine that was failing me when I needed it more than ever. These violent words. *Letdown. Trigger. Latch.* I particularly hated *trigger* and *latch*. Perhaps because I associate *trigger* with guns, the quiet-loud click of cold steel. Also, *trigger* as the meaningful revealing of information, information that requires a sombre announcement, before the bad news lands. *Latch* as lock, containment, cruelty. But also *latch* from the Old English *læccan*: "to grasp or seize, catch hold of — but also, to comprehend."

I was far from comprehending why my body wouldn't perform the way I wanted it to perform. I foisted my unwieldy breast into Cole's mouth countless times. Nothing worked. I cried. He cried. No latching, and yet I stubbornly refused to feed him formula. I had read too many brainwashing articles about the importance of breast milk. I just had to make my body function, perform, provide.

I frantically made appointments with every lactation specialist in town who would meet with me. My calendar was rife with red circles. Jane at eleven a.m., Karen at four p.m.

Confident white women paraded through our filthy apartment, filthy because we were too tired to clean it. One came in wearing a clingy strapless terry cloth jumpsuit in an electric-salmon colour, her breasts swollen like pendulums. I was envious both of her outfit and the seeming source of her sustenance.

Cole screamed. I winced from the pain.

Still no latch.

My mom told me that she'd had no problems breastfeeding. She told me quietly, as if she didn't want to tell me.

We were all flummoxed. Why was this happening?

My friend Brenda told me that this was, ultimately, about my relationship with my mother. Until I resolved my mothering issues, Cole would not latch. But how to resolve them? What could I do? I was angry with my mother for not visiting me, for not spending more time with Cole. But I knew it was a long trek for her from Markham to Toronto. I couldn't ask so much . . .

I feel angry with myself for writing that now, even if it's the truth.

Bruce and I finally procured an appointment with a vaunted doctor near North York General. He was legendary in Toronto for getting people to breastfeed. My mother drove on the dreaded Highway 401, her nemesis, to bring me to him. We travelled from the gleaming glass towers of the city to the manicured shamrock-green lawns of North York. When we got to the hospital, the doctor peered into Cole's mouth and immediately declared, "I have to cut your son's tongue."

Sleep-deprived, I didn't question him. I thought hazily, *Yes, yes, whatever it takes. Do it.* I don't remember saying this out loud. I must have, though. Didn't I?

He took out a pair of shiny scissors, separated Cole's dewy lips with his heavy fingers. Snipped a section just below Cole's tongue — and said something about how this would make it easier for Cole to latch.

There was blood. Not too much. Less than I expected. But more than I wanted.

The difference wasn't magical. But over the next few days, Cole latched.

The thread of the trauma of the ancestors, detached now, tongue freed. Is that what happened? I wondered at the time: will he now be able to speak, as I have not?

Shingles II

The shingles became excruciatingly painful. I booked appointment after appointment to see specialist after specialist. The agonizing nerve pain reverberated across my back, left shoulder and armpit. The oozing patches of red were slowly healing, but the pain remained.

My mother called, her daily check-in. "*Beti*, how is your shingles?"

"Fine, Mom, so much better," I lied.

Her own pain was getting worse. I could hear her words starting to slur. My brother had told me her mouth was beginning to froth, white foam appearing in the corners, deadly bubbles.

"Mucositis occurs when cancer treatments break down the rapidly divided epithelial cells lining the gastro-intestinal tract (which goes from the mouth to the anus), leaving the mucosal tissue open to ulceration and infection," explained the Oral Cancer Foundation website.

She didn't need to know about my pain. She was going through enough.

I booked appointments every day after the radio show, leaving the station promptly at noon to see a traditional Chinese medicine doctor forty-five minutes away at Oakridge Centre. My producers would call out to me about the next day's show as I rushed to pack up my things. "Sure, sure," I would respond, heading for the door. No one knew why I exited the building so quickly, and I didn't want anyone to know. The pain was often so bad while I interviewed that I tried to breathe into it, counting slowly until it subsided: *one Mississippi, two Mississippi . . .* I would also count the hours, minutes, seconds before I could leave.

When I arrived at the doctor's office for my requisite needling one afternoon, a few weeks in, he inspected the scars that were beginning to appear across my chest.

"It's getting better, and it's getting worse," he pronounced.

"What do you mean? Aren't I getting better?" *I must be getting better.*

He didn't say a word. I could see he was expecting me to think what he was thinking. Then finally he said, "Your anxiety is still so high. You have to find a way to cut down on your stress."

He knew about my mom, my job in radio, and he was trying to tell me to back out of everything. I could feel my anxiety reverberating on the cold steel table. All the poking and pricking and the potions he was making me drink wouldn't do a thing unless I released the pain myself.

But I wasn't sure I wanted to.

The truth was that I wasn't deserving of good health when she didn't seem to be.

An Uneasy Truce

It was December 2015. My mom's prognosis was poor. I was back in Vancouver, but always on my mind was my next trip to Toronto, where I could be with her. Meanwhile, I tried to be as present with my guests as I could, while my heart was elsewhere and the shingles continued to bother me. Even at such a tender age, or maybe because of it, Cole could sense something was wrong. I was cross with him more than I should have been. I checked my horoscope daily, and when it didn't tell me what I longed to hear, I convinced myself I'd read it wrong.

Don and I grabbed a drink at the now-defunct hipster restaurant Chill Winston, mere minutes from the radio station in Gastown, for a quick critique of my recent work. Despite our differences, of which there were many, I was starting to hold a begrudging admiration for him. After all, he had been in the business for years, and I was still a newbie. He still barked orders at me on occasion, but he was almost always right.

He was a high school dropout. (Actually, that's not true. I would find out later he got a GED to get into the US Army Security Agency.) He grew up in a working-class family near Pittsburgh and served during Vietnam. These details had been dispensed to me rather slowly, over several glasses of wine in the last few months.

At Chill Winston, Don downed his drink as per usual. I worked hard to keep up, drinking the rosé he ordered for me, but I was still a lightweight, despite my late nights of drinking port with my graduate school friends in London. We were talking ratings, and what I still needed to do with my voice, my sound, to improve. I still spoke too fast. Some interviews were too long. The show needed to pick up the pace. I was better, but it was still not good enough. I took notes with my Sheaffer fountain pen, which I'd had since I was a child. Comfort in crisis. Then he said suddenly, "You'll be proud of me. You know what someone said to me today about your show?"

"No, what?"

"This guy I know, he said to me, 'That show of Minelle's. I gotta tell you, why doesn't she have more white men on? I mean, it's biased. She should have more people on like you. Too many Brown people. Know what I'm sayin'?'"

Don paused for effect, then grinned. "Wait till you hear what I told him. I said, 'Don't you think we've heard enough from people like me? Enough with the old white guys.' I knew you'd be proud of me." He laughed.

I sat back in my chair, astonished. But I tried not to look it. What was I supposed to say? Was I supposed to be grateful? In a strange way, I was. I was relieved. I was relieved to be relieved.

Did this mean I would get to keep my job?

Hate Mail

It won't be a surprise, then, that other complaints came in about my perspective being biased. *Biased*, that awful word. Not a lot, but a few here and there. For every ten letters congratulating us on the uniqueness of *Sense of Place*, we got one complaint, sometimes even hate mail. It was the hate mail that garnered attention from Don.

I interviewed a former white supremacist on the show. I'd assumed it would be a run-of-the-mill interview exploring his turn to the other side. But his tone grew more and more aggressive with me over the course of the interview. During the break, off air, he made a few derogatory comments about Muslims and people of colour. No one else heard him because his mic was off. I started to cry at the end of the interview, my voice breaking — I was praying no listeners would catch it. Don looked up from his desk and saw the furious posture of the former white supremacist as he stormed out of the studio. My boss became deeply concerned, said he couldn't sleep because of it and started to investigate getting a security detail for me. We were all glad that the studio was encased in bulletproof glass. "Who knew that would come in handy," Don said.

I developed heart palpitations when I went to work. I hyperventilated as soon as I opened the heavy glass doors to the building. My hands started to shake again during interviews. I kept them down on the desk, hoping no one would see them fluttering.

Prayers over the Placenta

I was forty-two years old when I gave birth to my little boy, my heart's desire.

When my placenta was dislodged from my body, it was my mom, not my partner, who was by my side. Bruce had done everything he could to fly to Toronto as quickly as he possible, but he didn't make it in time. We were still long-distance during my pregnancy, holding university jobs in our respective cities: I was teaching in Toronto, and Bruce in Vancouver. He visited often, but this was one flight that couldn't be booked in advance. Cole arrived two weeks early.

So, it was my mother who, along with my oldest friend Joylyn, helped me push out the baby.

They fed me melting ice chips and crunchy marbled cheese straws, my favourite, during labour. The actual labour turned out not to be laboured at all, I am grateful to say. What I remember about that time is this: My mother insisted on keeping the placenta. I was too hopped up on adrenalin and the epidural rush to care much about her request. If she wanted it, she could have it. What need did I have for it, anyway? She didn't tell me why she wanted it. I would find it later in her freezer when I was rummaging around for a pint of Häagen-Dazs.

A few months later, it was spring and the daffodils were pushing up out of the ground in her garden. She was very proud of her garden and rightly so: it was a beauty. When I arrived, baby in tow, she was digging in the back lot, and I could see the frozen placenta sweating copiously in a clear plastic bag on the soil next to a flower bed.

I asked her what on earth she was doing.

"I am conducting a ritual. I'm going to plant this placenta in this earth. Ruth is coming over, and we are going to do a ceremony here, right here, over the placenta."

As if on cue, Ruth, her neighbour, strode into the garden, her Bible firmly under her arm. Ruth was religious, Catholic, I think. In turn, my mom brought out her threadbare old Quran. Together, they placed the placenta delicately into the earth, bowing their heads, murmuring quiet prayers, one in English, the other in Arabic, like a musical duet.

To this day, I wonder if the placenta is still in the ground, in her garden. I sold her house after she died, and sometimes I regret not digging it out and keeping it. But wouldn't that have been the ultimate colonial act — to sloppily unearth it, just to claim it, to own it, rather than allow its tendrils to spread, take root, so other plants could grow?

Live from Railtown

I didn't tell any of my radio guests that my mother was dying. I tried not to mention it to my co-workers, although the ones who'd experienced significant loss saw through me and their expressions told me so.

The music director, Cory, the experienced DJ I'd met on my first day at Roundhouse, was one of those people. He mentioned in passing that his dad had died but didn't elaborate. I didn't ask any questions. I couldn't take any more stories about grief. And, frankly, I was intimidated by him, by all the pros with years of experience behind the mic. I watched in awe as he seamlessly took over from me after each shift. He was always upbeat and charming on air. "*Live from Railtown!*" he boomed into the mic as I rushed out of the studio to another acupuncture appointment, making space for him.

When I heard that Matthew Good would be coming in for a studio interview, I begged Cory to let me do it. It was a source of embarrassment to my family, my adoration of this particular rock star who mostly appealed to white men in their twenties. I was often the only person at his concerts not clad in a plaid flannel shirt and baseball cap. I didn't care. I was done making excuses for my bad taste in music. He was my favourite, and that was that.

When I asked Cory if he would let me interview Good, he gave me a bit of side-eye. Everyone knew not to let me "do music" at the station. But then he agreed. Victory! I was ecstatic, until I discovered that one of my mother's most important consultations with the ENT specialist would occur on the same day in Toronto. I knew she would want me there. Inwardly, I groaned. I couldn't do the interview. I told Cory so, and he just shrugged, said nothing. He would do it, and I knew he would do it well. But I was disappointed.

When I returned from Toronto after a consult that offered us little reason for optimism, I walked into the office to find the brand new CD by Matthew Good on my desk. On it, scribbled in thick black Sharpie, was "To Minelle — From Matthew Good."

I skipped over to Cory's desk, beaming. "Cory, thank you! How did you get this from him! He's notoriously difficult to get an autograph from!" I'd done the preliminary research and knew Good's distaste for fandom.

Cory was sorting CDs, stacks and stacks of them. The clicking of the jewel cases stopped, and he smiled.

"Don't worry about it," he said, shrugging. "No big deal." He went back to organizing; Said the Whale, Billy Bragg CDs flipped by me.

I remembered the vague knowledge I held about his own father's passing. It *was* a big deal, and with my expression, I told him so.

These small generous gestures. They took my breath away.

Sons and Daughters

Sometimes men call those who are not their biological sons *son*. I hear them do this in bait and tackle shops, at athletic stores, at the hockey arena. It can be an endearment, a tenderness, not always a description of a specific biological relationship. A different kind of kinship.

I don't know of an equivalent for women. Women do not call those who are not their daughters *daughter*. The colloquial use of *son* has a particular cadence and currency unbeknownst to *daughter*.

Why is that?

When I hear *son* used in this way, it fills me with warmth — as if such radical reciprocity could be possible.

How can we write with a different lexicon — to have a more affectionate and luscious language at our fingertips? How can we learn to speak in a way that acknowledges our relationships with our women ancestors, our women mentors, with the women to whom we offer mentorship?

In this world, I would call my mother *daughter*.

And maybe she would call me *mother* too.

The Geography of Time

Hours, minutes, seconds. They all seemed to be taking on eerie new proportions, casting greater spectres, feeling more potent and poignant with every passing day. Time felt so fraught to me. The questions, again: How much time do I have left with her? Will she get the surgery next week, next month, next year? What does *terminal* mean, and when does it begin and end?

Will this story have a happy ending?

The thing about being a radio host was that you knew your interview would always end. There was always a beginning, a middle and an end. You had a finite amount of time. It's what you and your guest do with the time you have together that matters. That's what radio gave me ultimately: a different understanding of how to manipulate time and its multiple geographies. To recognize its sprawling expanse one minute, then to notice I was stuck in a constricted space the next.

I am laughing as I read this now — I like the way I just wrote that sentence, as if I was the one who manipulated time. As if I ever had that much control over its cartography. I suppose I was reluctant to state the truth of the matter, which is that time actually manipulated me.

I was at the mercy of time. Trying to figure out tone and how to move from interview to interview with ease stymied me. So much depended on the intros — the way I introduced a guest. I wanted to do this with both care and compassion. My intros became living eulogies — broken tributes to people who were still lucky enough to breathe. I think I was trying to keep my mother alive by writing eulogies for my guests who were still living. I threaded together every single sacred thing I could about them to animate and loudly announce their existences. I was trying to speak them into being, even when they were sitting right across from me, all blood and breath and body.

"Minelle, your intros are too long," the consultant told me. Chuck was his name. He was a country-western guy, bald but in that cool way, with a smile that could light up a city skyline. He mostly worked at country stations, but for some reason, he was assigned to work with me every week, teaching me how to do radio. And over meals, he would tell me, *You're putting too much into your intros.*

Tell me something I don't know, cowboy.

PART FOUR

QUESTIONS AND ANSWERS

"Do not now seek the answers, which cannot be given to you because you would not be able to live them. And the point is, to live everything. *Live* the questions now. Perhaps you will then gradually, without noticing it, live . . . into the answer."

— RAINER MARIA RILKE, *Letters to a Young Poet*

Frankfurt

My mother got worse.

When I flew back to Toronto again, I discovered with shock that her clothing now billowed around her tiny body. She was emaciated. She could no longer chew. We started to rely on texting, hand gestures over FaceTime to communicate. Mere months after her diagnosis, she could no longer talk.

It all felt so helpless, hopeless when we heard nothing back from the hospital about treatment options. We waited for radiation appointments to be booked, but nothing . . .

The silence told us all we needed to know. In the face of it all, I realized I had no options left. I had exhausted all the hospitals, begged for second, third opinions; called up friends who were doctors, cajoling them to call their friends for help; left messages at other clinics where we were left constantly *waiting . . . waiting . . . waiting . . .* for a call that would never come, waiting for the date of the operation that we knew would come too late. I was left scrounging around for hope in all the wrong places. And so the ever-faithful researcher started googling again.

Sure enough those clever algorithms detected my distress. In my Facebook feed, the ads found me, sensing my despair. I hungrily read a post by someone who claimed that his wife's cancer was eliminated through a short but pricey stint at a clinic in Germany. Infusio, it was called. Their logo was a tidy sprig of green leaves, very much like what you'd expect a dove to carry in its mouth. I was entranced by this man's story — it was so seductive, his post, and I felt I had stumbled upon something important.

I obsessively researched the clinic. It had two locations: one in Frankfurt, one in Beverly Hills. I looked at both; Beverly Hills was closer, but they didn't offer cancer treatment. The reviews hypnotized me. They were rife with gold stars and exclamation marks, riddled with relief.

I was convinced this was our solution, our reprieve, and I rushed to tell Ray. God had led me to this clinic, and it held our salvation. My brother, however, was more dubious. I buckled in — I was going to convince him.

I tracked down the writer of the Facebook post and sent him a pleading message, asking if we could chat on the phone. He said yes. He was in California; I was in Toronto at my mother's house. Mom was sleeping on the couch, a peeling pink leather monstrosity I had always hated. Her body looked so fragile and perfect against that pathetic piece of furniture that I was even more certain this was the right decision. With my brother's two cats swirling around his legs, mewling, and my mother scarcely able to move, I dialed the number and took a deep breath.

"Stuart? I'm calling about the clinic — my mom and brother are on speakerphone," I said breathlessly. *Pleasehavetheanswers-pleasehavetheanswers-pleasehavetheanswers.*

Stuart was in sparkling Los Angeles, and his voice sounded as sunny as I wanted my family to be. We were, ourselves, freezing, even with the heat cranked up. The wind outside whirled with a particular viciousness that winter, blizzards incessantly pelting the roof with snow. Stuart spoke with certainty about why the clinic was the best in the world. How it had cured his wife's cancer and how it would most certainly do the same for us. His compliments echoed what I had seen on Infusio's website: simple, sophisticated photos;

sparkling white, modern, clean, pure lines; endless promises of good health and, of course, excellent, excellent results. The very best!

As Stuart spoke, I could see my mom trying so hard to pay attention, but she kept dozing off, exhausted by merely trying to listen. She had heard empty promises from far too many people. But Stuart's voice — it held so much certainty. Except when it came to costs. He mentioned something about Infusio being "worth every dollar."

My brother was only slightly more reassured after the phone call. But the next day I sent an email to the clinic, asking if they could admit her by late December. I received a reply the very next day: they did have a spot on December 15. We were so fortunate. So lucky! Someone had dropped out. The treatment would take a month. They did not speak in terms of cure, of course, but they knew that that is what I expected. It would cost twenty-five thousand US dollars.

It was an exorbitant amount of money.

The next day, in hushed tones while our mother snored sweetly on the couch, my brother and I looked at our bank accounts to see what we could manage. Could we max out all our credit cards and push up her line of credit? But the financial struggle was not the only question on our minds. Could we actually do it? What would it be like to take her to Germany? Could she handle the trip? We hurled questions at one another, never recognizing the futility of our faith.

Neither of us had ever been to Germany. We did a vague mock-up of the costs to travel there, for all three of us to go. The good news was that the twenty-five grand included the cost of the apartment above the clinic where our mother would stay. The bad news was that my brother and I would have to get our own apartment.

We looked at the figures again and grappled with the estimated costs. Again, exorbitant. But what else could we do? There was a solution to this problem, and I was convinced this was it. And now my brother was too.

When my mother's eyes fluttered open, my brother and I cleared our throats and made our case like we were lawyers who knew their client was guilty. We said this could be a success story. We said this place has cured cancer for others. Why not her? *This is what will save you*, we said without saying it.

I'm embarrassed to tell you that I can't fully recall her response. Was she jubilant about going? Was she trepidatious, scared, skeptical? All I remember is a vacant look in her eyes. And she tried to reassure both of us.

She would go for us, even if she didn't want to go.

I found a website that booked first-class tickets at almost reasonable prices. I just couldn't fathom flying my mother economy, her bones so brittle, her birdlike body barely able to handle a wheelchair. I had so much regret about never having flown her first class when her body was still healthy, when she could have appreciated the experience in a more sensual, in a fully sensory, way. Now it was merely a means of trying to keep her safe. We made the plans. My brother would accompany her to Frankfurt while I flew home to Vancouver, said hello to my son and partner and finished up another week of radio before joining Mom and Ray for most of the holiday break. The station would be closed, so Don wouldn't have to find someone to fill in for me. Then on Christmas Eve, I would fly to Florida to meet up with my child and partner in Miami, where Bruce's family lived, to spend a few days with them. A raft of tickets was booked: YVR to ZRH to FRA.

I was not sure what to put in my mother's suitcase. I threw in a few velour nightgowns, her *tasbih*, her prayer book. Her entire wardrobe reeked of thieves oil now. The irony of that phrase — the thieves had stolen everything from her, including her voice, and yet she continued to plaster the naturopathic ointment she got from Owen all over her gums.

Even today, I become nauseous and can't stand to be near the scent when I walk into a natural food store.

A few weeks later, at the Vancouver airport, I was feeling overwhelmed and anxious ahead of my flight to Frankfurt. To distract myself, I browsed the jewellery kiosks. I felt like I needed something to hold me down, something to keep me grounded. I looked at many pieces — gold bracelets that looked like shiny yellow straw, pearl earrings. But then I came across something. It was a tiny silver feather on a thin chain. A symbol of flight and freedom.

I didn't wait for the cashier to put it in a box. I took it immediately after paying and placed it around my neck. The second I did, I felt safer, closer to the ground.

Flanked Bird

I was thirty-eight and living with Blake, that boyfriend I would eventually leave. He's less important to this particular story. We were fostering a stray cat. It was my hope that the cat would make our house a home, but no number of felines could take away the chill that enveloped our forlorn four-bedroom house in the Beaches. Despite my crooning overtures, the cat kept declining my affection. It remained standoffish. In revenge, I childishly refused to name it, but Blake decided to call it Noodle and it stuck.

Noodle arrived proudly at our bed one morning, clenching a sparrow in his jaws, feathers sprouting from his mouth. I admonished the cat, and the bird dropped to the hardwood floor. Noodle rushed away.

The bird lay there, quivering with fear.

I gingerly picked it up, its breast barely beating. It was tiny, delicate. It was clearly hurt, and it needed help — but what could we do? Take it to the animal hospital? Would they even admit it?

Panicked, I went online and found a wilderness centre near Leslie and Finch, a little outside the city. They said they would see the bird — but not until the next day.

Blake said to forget it, there was no hope for it. Odd, because I knew he loved to take wounded birds under his wing.

But I was up in arms about the bird. I wheedled on the phone. *It needs help now, please, please see it today.* I had no car, but I was determined to get that bird up to Leslie and Finch somehow to keep it alive. But they were adamant, telling me again, *No, not possible.* I would have to find a way to keep its heart beating for another day on my own.

I found a cardboard box, put an old red checked blanket inside and placed the bird carefully on it. I tried to keep the sparrow warm. Its chest beat up, down, scarcely perceptible.

I searched my bookshelves and flanked the box with two books. I tilted the Quran heavily on one side of the box. On the other, the Bhagavad-Gita. On one side, the history of my mother; the other side, my father. Between the covers ran the gamut of goodness. A lopsided altar.

When Blake saw these heavy tomes bookending the box, he guffawed. "You're ridiculous! You really think *that* will save it?" He mumbled something about needing a Bible in there for good measure as he walked away. "There's no hope for that bird."

Of course he was right. And yet I did it anyway. I left the books there overnight. The bird died the next day, on the way to the clinic. The two books proved useless, powerless against a larger force unbeknownst to me.

The Vestibule

This is the story I didn't want to tell you. You have stories like that, too, right? Stories you want to keep hidden? I didn't want to tell you because I don't want or need your pity.

I was twenty-three years old and had recently started my PhD at University College London. I was late for a casual dinner party in Hampstead Heath with new friends I had met from my part-time job at the Gap. There was a chill in the late October air. I was wearing a dirty and scuffed CBC *Newsworld* baseball cap and my oversized royal-blue Mountain Equipment Co-op windbreaker. I was carrying a salt-and-vinegar Pringles tin full of chocolate chip cookies I had just baked. The tin felt cozy-warm in my hands.

I was breathless, rushing, running out the elevator door of my apartment in Kentish Town when two large men loudly burst into the foyer. Not the main lobby, but the tiny space before it with the intercom. I tried to walk around them, but the vestibule was tight, unyielding. They grabbed me, lifted me up and, *bam*, slammed my body against the cement wall. The cookies flew out of the container, dancing through the air. They held me suspended. Time stopped. I heard nothing.

Then sound came to me — their guttural laughter, knife-edged, scalpel-sharp — and the smell of a pint or three on their breath.

I was paralyzed. I tried to call for her — *Mama* — but no sound came out. I tried to scream but couldn't.

After what seemed like an interminable amount of time, they dropped me to the ground. I tried to run out of the building, but they were blocking the front door. They were laughing; I couldn't make out what they were saying. I rushed back into the building instead and started to pound on apartment doors, screaming — or was I screaming? I don't know if my voice came out.

"Help me! Help me!" I think I whisper-screamed. No one came to see what the noise was about, to discover why someone was banging on their door. I kept running, banging, maybe screaming, door after door after door. There was no way out, no exit. I was trapped. Panting at the end of the long corridor, I curled up on the cold hard ground.

Eventually, I can't say after how long, I managed to pick myself up. I slowly walked to the front door of my building. No one was there. They had gone.

I walked to the Tube station shaking.

I finally arrived at my friend's house, to eat with the four lovely men who worked with me at the Gap. We had a beautiful dinner, cooked lovingly on a cracked hot plate in student housing. The narrow room was crowded and warm. We devoured what was left of the cookies. Some had miraculously stayed in the container. I didn't say anything until we were all luxuriously sipping on cheap whiskey out of crappy striped mugs at the end of the night.

"S-something happened to me. On my way here." I wasn't sure what to say. I stammered out the story. *I only got thrown up against the wall*, I thought. *Maybe it isn't a big deal. Maybe they didn't know better.*

If I was a guy, I could have handled it.

My friend Theo listened thoughtfully. I could see what he was thinking. His eyes asked, *Are you okay?* And his expression answered: *You're not okay. I can see you're not okay.*

Ben blustered, "Let's go back there now. I'll beat the hell out of those guys!"

I reassured them. I'm fine, *I'm fine, no damage done. Really.*

After dinner, I returned to the apartment on my own, no longer my apartment, of course. I'd lost ownership in that moment. I went back on my own despite my friends' insistence that I stay with them, insistence that I required an accompanying larger force.

I was relieved to find the foyer empty. I spotted two of the errant cookies, one in the corner, another under the radiator, crushed. I thought about cleaning them up but decided to let it be. I got into the apartment unscathed, key in lock, door firmly shut, *click*, my body on the safe side of the door now.

Afterwards, whenever a man brushed by me on the sidewalk, my heart raced. I started exiting the building by the side door to avoid the foyer.

I decided to abandon London, never admitting to anyone, my mother, myself, why I was really leaving. I told myself it was because I was out of money, but that wasn't the real truth of it. I just didn't feel safe in the city any longer. I had to get out.

I never pressed charges, never went to the police, never told anyone apart from my friends at the dinner that night. I never had to act as a witness, never had to take the stand, never had to speak to a single constable. I stayed silent. It wasn't a rape, it wasn't an assault, right? It wasn't anything. I kept saying this to myself. My voice did not help me that night, or the next day, or the day after.

It Was at a Party

"It happened at a party," she whispered almost conspiratorially as I slurped on my Kwality Ice Cream vanilla shake, the soothing cold drink coating my throat. She bent her head toward me. I was sixteen. We had just visited the Oxford Bookstore on Park Street in Kolkata, near her old high school, and had ducked into this coffee shop for a drink. We were on the trip we took without my father.

"It was at a party," she repeated.

What she told me:

Her mother, dazzlingly decked out in a sparkling sari, embroidered with fuchsia and gold, and a twenty-four-karat necklace with matching curtain earrings. Her father, in a jacket with a crisp Nehru neckline, greeting guests with panache, pouring just a bit of extra whiskey into the men's glasses with a wink. The tinkling of crystal, the guests accepting the *shami kababs* served on silver trays.

She got tired of gazing up at all the guests and finally asked her mother, tugging on her sari, if she could leave.

"Yes, *beti*, go, go," her mother said impatiently, scanning the room to make sure her guests felt welcome. My mother scampered out the door, into the guest house. She sat in that cold and cramped room, grateful for the respite.

A few minutes later, the door creaked open.

"It was one of the guests, a friend of my parents, someone I did not know," she said, her voice wavering. "I did know him, a little, maybe, but I didn't know him."

I felt the weight of her words. I stopped slurping on my milkshake and looked at her. Tears in her eyes.

"He said, 'Come here, sweetie, I just want to say hi.'"

She approached him tentatively in her tiny party dress, with the polka dots and the blue satin collar. She was four years old. He offered her his hand.

"I felt I had no choice but to take it."

Her hands on the Formica tabletop now trembled. I covered her beautiful fingers with my own, layered my hands over hers. I said nothing.

She was four.

"He took me into the bedroom and told me it would be okay."

Shewasfour-shewasfour-shewasfour.

I need not tell you the rest. You know what happened next. But I did not know, at the time, and I asked her to tell me and I wish I had not asked. One question I absolutely regret asking, in stark contrast to the many I did not ask that I now wish I had.

"It's not your fault, Mom. It's not . . ." I said. I gripped her hands tightly.

"I know, Muni. I know. I just wanted you to know."

Christmastime in Germany

When I flew to Frankfurt to be by her side in December, sporting my new feather necklace, my carry-on stuffed with shingles medications, a new brand of dread consumed me. I couldn't bear to be on that plane, couldn't bear to go where I was going. And in the dread, I found myself doing something I had never done before. I decided I would pray on the floor of the plane, visible for all to see. Did I want to do this because a Muslim family in first class had just done so and this helped me muster up enough courage to do the same?

I walked toward the toilets tentatively and knelt down. The family in first class saw me and, realizing I had no hijab, lent me their beige satin head covering. Before I got off the plane, they gave it to me to keep. I was moved by their generosity. I still use it sometimes, the smoothness of the fabric calming.

The drive to the clinic from the Frankfurt airport felt long. My mother lay in bed, thinner than I'd ever seen her. She couldn't speak anymore. But she smiled. Luminescent.

The clinic was white, brisk and clean. Every morning, a new procedure was foisted upon my mother: a healthy regimen, they told us. Either a vitamin IV or an injection of a new medicine or some sort of laser procedure — all of which I blindly trusted.

My mother gestured to the clinicians, then pointed to me. "Please help my daughter's shingles," she scribbled on a pad of paper.

I told my mom, no, no, we can't afford any more treatments, but she insisted. They placed me on a medical table, and I received a series of five injections all the way down my back. The procedure cost about a thousand dollars. The injections ultimately did nothing, though, and now all I have to show for them are five small scars, pockmarks like buttons all the way down my back, a kind of straitjacket.

Frankfurt the city was all beer steins and sausages and perpetual darkness even during midday, and my mother clutching my arm as she carefully navigated the wet cobblestone streets on the rare occasion she had the energy for a short walk. How she looked away with sadness as I ordered yet another beer. How I tried to get her to drink more of that bone broth laden with organic root vegetables they served in the clinic in a meagre attempt to make her stronger. The wretched rain that fell each and every goddamned day.

I knew in my heart that I would never, ever go back to that city again.

What do I choose to remember from that time?

What prayers can I say now? What prayers can I say, now?

Khao-swe

Another question for you. A more cheerful one. I told you this isn't just a sad story, right? What's your favourite food?

My guess is it's something your mother made for you. Or a close relative. Perhaps it's something you associate with a cherished relationship. Is this why they call it comfort food?

When my mother became ill, a thought kept gnawing at me. *Will she ever cook for me again?* Even though she wasn't gone yet, with a macabre practicality, I wondered if I would be able to find some frozen delicacies she had put aside at her home. I felt guilty thinking this, but I was already in the after in some ways.

In the days before Frankfurt, I scoured my mother's house for recipes. Her delicious shrimp curry, her spicy chicken divan . . . But there was one particular dish I was looking for, the one that held a place of pride in our family: my mother's *ohn no khao-swe*.

Egg noodles studded with cubed boneless chicken, dotted with hard-boiled eggs, *dhania* (cilantro), lemon, chilis and scallions. *Khao-swe* originated from Burma, where my mother's parents had been based for several years. This dish had travelled from Burma to Iran with them, and now with us to North America. Always served at our family holidays and gatherings. Emails from my cousins: "I can't wait for Christmas dinner . . . is Ameh making *khao-swe*?"

But I couldn't find the recipe anywhere.

When I'd studied in Chapel Hill and my mom had come to visit, I'd asked her to write the recipe into my journal. In her beautiful writing, and with perfect curlicues and doodles framing the page, she'd captured the recipe, closing it with a stylized "Bon Appetit!!!!!" It was more artwork than recipe. But where was that journal?

I found a recipe for *khao-swe* on a Burmese website and did my best to recreate it, but it was only mediocre. What is it about the addition of this or that, a pinch of something we have forgotten that so changes the taste of a food we have deep affection for? Would I ever be able to recreate it?

I placed the dish in front of Cole to see what he thought. He devoured it, much to my surprise. I thought about what I'd read in *The Guardian* earlier that day: that a child's food preferences begin in the womb and that tests have shown that what a person eats during their pregnancy is easily detectable in their amniotic fluid. The fetus develops a taste for familiar flavours.

Maybe it was in his DNA to love it as much as I do.

A Quick Story about Dogs

I didn't really know where to put this story. But it feels about right to say that this story needs a story about dogs, not just because I believe every story should have a story about dogs but also because dogs in this story matter.

And doesn't almost every story about dogs tell another story too? One that is not really about dogs per se, but about something else entirely.

So another question for you:

Do you know what haram is? If you are Muslim, you do.

Haram is anything that goes against the will of God. You know, anything that is evil or wrong. A few things that are haram: pork, alcohol and — according to my mother — dogs.

Dogs are not allowed in a Muslim household, my mother would tell us over and over. Dogs are disgusting, gross, impure and unsanitary. Do you see the way they lick their private parts? And they smell revolting? *Astaghfirullah*. No, you are never, ever getting a dog. End. Of. Story. And that is that.

My mother clung to this belief — until my dad died.

In the last year of his life, my dad procured a shih tzu puppy. Remember I mentioned he had one? Zippy and clever, white with butterscotch markings, Simone sported a tiny rhinestone-studded collar. My dad adored this puppy, this loud-mouthed little thing. I had no use for her — you might be surprised to learn, given my sentimentality, that I was inured to puppies. This would dramatically change years later when I got my own dog.

When my dad's lifeless body was found in his apartment, the dog was by his side, yapping impatiently by the bed. For years, I couldn't stop thinking about that poor dog, bounding up and down next to my dad's cold body — that wee puppy, eagerly and anxiously saying *Get up! Get up! Get up!* and never getting a response.

After my dad's body was removed from his apartment, nobody knew what to do with the dog. I couldn't take her; my building didn't allow dogs. My brother lived with my mother. He could take the dog. But my mom — she hated dogs. Dogs were haram. My brother implored, "Please, please."

And she looked at the creature, at that yapping loud thing, and said reluctantly, "Yes, yes, we will take it."

But what happened next was a surprise. Instead of merely tolerating the puppy, she grew to love her in a way that none of us could have expected — especially my mom.

She would call me and ask thousands of questions about the dog.

"Minelle, what kind of treats do you think the dog would like? I don't want to give the dog pork treats, but the dog would like the pork treats, right? Haram!"

"*Junam*, I want to get the dog groomed but at a nice place that will make the dog look beautiful — where should I go?"

"Muni, you won't believe what the dog did today. Did you know she rolled over when I gave her a treat? *Mashallah*, you are so cute. Aren't you cute, *junam* dog?"

The dog became an extension of her. Simone accompanied her to her school every day and sat by her feet in her office. The students delighted in rubbing Simone's small body, and she basked in their attention.

And then one day, I got the phone call. It was about three months after my dad's death, and I was still wincing every time the phone rang. I'd been about to head over to the lecture hall to teach a class about feminist geographies and was absent-mindedly pulling on a pair of teal suede heels when she called.

"Muni, Muni!" my mom screamed down the phone. She sounded terrified, breathless.

"What, what, Mom?" I panicked. "Is Ray okay? Has there been an accident?" I took a deep breath. *I can't go through this again, not so soon. Not now.*

"Yes, someone is dying!" she wailed.

An image of my brother, his body battered in his silver Honda Civic, appeared in my mind. I saw the crushed steering wheel, the car like crumpled tinfoil.

"Mom, Mom, is Ray okay? What happened? What happened? Is it Ray?" *Please God, let it not be Ray. Anything but Ray.*

"No, no, it's not Ray. It's the dog! The dog is dying!"

"What do you mean, Mom? Tell me! Slow down! What is happening?"

"The dog is dying! The dog is dying!" she repeated, screaming.

My heart in my throat. "Mom, just take a deep breath. Tell me. Tell me what is going on."

"THE DOG IS CHOKING ON A PIECE OF CHEESE!"

My mother had given the dog a treat — a wedge of white cheddar that Simone coveted more than anything. But if you have a shih tzu, you know that their mouths are very, very small. As ever, my mother wanted to please the thing and give her what she wanted, but she gave her way too much.

"Mom, fish it out — get your finger in there! Pull it out!" *Please, please save Simone*, I prayed.

I heard her drop the phone as she cajoled the creature. "*Junam, junam*, please listen to me," she begged. "Let it go, let it go." I could hear the dog yelping, shuffling, more noise.

The phone went silent. Then she came back on the line, her voice heavy, ragged.

"The dog, the dog — the dog is dead," she said. "She's stopped breathing, *junam*. She's dead."

We sat on the phone for a minute, not saying a word to each other but knowing the other was there.

Was it really possible the dog was dead — from choking on a piece of cheese? I didn't know what to do. It was two minutes to class and so I told my mom I had to go. I gave a two-hour lecture on Gillian Rose and paradoxical space, but I don't remember anything I said that day.

When I tried to comfort my mother later, I remembered an old Persian expression: when something gets stuck in your throat, you say "*pareed too galoom*" — پرید توگلوم — meaning "it jumped into my throat." You thus relieve yourself of any responsibility and place all the blame on the morsel of food. I told my mom this to make her feel better — *blame the food, not yourself, Mom!* — but she didn't believe me. She had taken that dog in and tried to give her a home. I said there was no way she could have known that a piece of cheese would kill her, but she just shook her head, tears in her eyes.

"I killed that dog," she would murmur. "I killed her."

I told her countless times that the dog wanted to be with my father, never sure that I really believed that. I'm not sure she ever forgave herself.

She buried that dog in her garden. Right near the place where she buried my placenta. That these two things are buried so close together brings me so much solace. I imagine the placenta offering a nest of care to the dog, as it did once for my son.

The Schloss

In the minuscule apartment we were renting in a suburb of Frankfurt, my mother was busy watching and rewatching videos of Cole that I had saved on my phone. She was smiling as he recited his Namaz perfectly into the camera. I had just taught him how to say the prayers before I had left. He had taken to wearing hijab just like me, insisted on it.

It was Saturday, the one day a week my mother didn't get treatments from the clinic. The doors shuttered, and so we were on our own, fending for ourselves in that chilly city. But it was her day off — her one day away from the countless needles, the many IV infusions. Could I pretend this was a day of tourism, fun and frolicking?

I could try.

"Mom, enough videos! Where do you want to go today?"

She looked at me, her eyes bright, and scribbled into her mini spiral notebook. "I want to go to the market to buy Cole a Christmas present."

I took a deep breath. I wasn't sure she would be able to take the crowds, the noise. The entire trip sounded exhausting. It was days before Christmas, and I was expecting a mad rush in downtown Frankfurt. But she looked at me, her doe eyes pleading, and it was all I could do to not say no. So we go.

I bundled her up as warmly as I could: faux-fur-lined winter boots, a down-filled coat. And we headed out the door, my brother, mother and I. The day was cold, but the milky winter sun peeked through the clouds. We made our way over to the black taxi waiting for us. The streets were not overwhelmingly busy. We asked the driver to take us to the shopping district, and he turned around in his seat.

"Oh, you want to go to the Schloss!" he said with enthusiasm in heavily accented English.

He was not white. This was somewhat of a relief—I'd been nervous my brother was going to face out-and-out racism while we were in Frankfurt because his skin was darker than mine. He never did, though, and later he chastised me for assuming that he would. *Minelle, you see racism everywhere.*

My brother and I looked at the driver, a little surprised by his exuberance.

"You know, the Christmas market!"

Suddenly I was drawn back into the novels of my childhood; a particular Madeleine L'Engle book came to mind where the main character went to what she called the Schloss and drank hot cider and purchased glass Christmas ornaments. With this dim recollection, I felt more buoyant.

He drove us directly into the square where the Christmas market was held. What we saw when we got there was a delight. It was a scene out of a Hallmark Christmas special of my dreams. There were majestic evergreens in the middle of the square, flanked by ornate buildings grandly laced up with twinkling white lights. Around us families were purchasing treasures from the train of market carts that were scattered around the square. Children sporting brick-red wool hats with pompoms ran around us in circles, trying to make snowballs out of the falling snow, catching snowflakes on their tongues.

This was my idea of heaven, and my mom's, too — we had always loved a good market. My brother had other ideas. I could feel him scowling next to me in the car, his leg agitating up against mine.

"Do we have to do this?" he moaned.

I remembered the time we went on a family trip — me, my mom and my brother — to Providence, Rhode Island. We took a family trip every year after my dad died. My mom and I decided to go to see *Eat, Pray, Love*, but my brother refused to come. *I ain't seeing that shit.* But my mother cajoled him into coming with us, and for the whole two hours in the theatre, all he did was fidget and squirm in his seat, utterly miserable.

"Yes, we do have to do this," I said, fending off the memory of the Rhode Island film disaster.

I could feel an inevitable fight brewing, sensing it coming toward me like a foreboding weather forecast.

My mother said nothing. She could feel it, too, though, I knew.

We got out of the car and started to peruse the stalls. My mother tentatively shuffled toward one, placed her shaking fingers between a beautiful embroidered magenta handkerchief and a thick crocheted sapphire shawl. I want to buy her everything, absolutely everything that made her eyes go wide. I feared it was her last time to buy anything, my last time to buy her anything — but she solemnly shook her head.

"No, no," she murmured to me, the sound emanating like a low hum from her mouth. It was all she could do now. Odd, this reversal to childhood sounds — moaning, humming, sighing, no language out of her mouth any longer, only murmurs, mumbles.

We stopped at a stall selling steaming mulled wine and apple cider in chipped mugs. The scent was inviting. My mouth watered. I stood in line and bought three cups. My brother grimaced upon taking a sip. "Gross," he declared.

My mother, always intrepid about trying new things, took a small sip and grimaced too.

Me? I gulped the thing down in two seconds. *Delicious.* I could feel the alcohol pulsing through me, warming up my bones.

My mother gestured toward a toy store across the square. *There, let's go there.*

"No, Mom, it'll be too crowded." I could see the crowds milling about in front of the store. It would be too much for her. But she shook her head vehemently. We would be going in and *that*, Muni, would be that.

"I'm not coming," my brother said.

I rolled my eyes. "Come on, just for a few seconds."

But my brother was not interested, said he would just wait outside. I tried not to argue, even though I was jonesing for a good fight. It would have made my day, month, year. *Bring it*, my jagged heart screamed.

I took my mother's arm, walked her into the store, and as expected, it was crowded. But my mother was not to be stopped. She immediately spotted an employee, a teenager in a store apron who was stacking the shelves with fluffy teddy bears. My mother scrawled on her pad of paper and handed it to me: "FIND THE TRAINS!"

My mother knew my son was obsessed with his wooden train set. She wanted to buy him a locomotive engine for his train. I marvelled at her memory, and then with a cruel pang, I realized it might be the last present she would purchase for her grandson.

I wandered over to the employee and somehow managed to convey to her in broken German that we were looking for the train accessories. She lead us over to the right section of the store, and my mother inspected the wares. After mulling over a few options she deemed lacklustre, she finally handed one to me. It was bright red, wooden and battery-operated, and it was exactly what my son would have loved. I could see in her eyes this was the one she wanted.

I took her arm again, and we headed to the cashier. I tried to pay, but she was too quick for me, despite the pain she was in, and she handed over her credit card. We walked out of the store, red locomotive in hand, and I could see she felt victorious. I allowed her to feel like she had accomplished something, and I thought maybe she had. I was in awe, wondering how the heck she could focus on her grandson's desires while she was clearly in so much pain. I saw it in every wince she made when she moved her mouth.

I have until this point not really spoken about the pain that tongue cancer causes, but believe me when I say doctors have told me that it is among the most painful cancers. The silvery-white foaming pus that appears near the end; the way the disease eats away at the tongue, creating tiny craters that make it look like the surface of the moon. I really didn't want to have to tell you the details. She refused to share what she was going through with me, with anyone.

Once outside the store, we searched for my brother. But he was nowhere to be found. It was crowded in the square, and there were many people milling about. I guided my mother to a bench and started looking for Ray, rushing into this shop and then another. In, out. In, out. Nothing. I worried about leaving my mother alone but kept going from store to store.

Nothing.

I became irate. I didn't think she had much left in her, and I imagined her yearning for her bed. I started calling out my brother's name, becoming more and more panicked. After searching for about ten minutes, I admitted defeat and plunked myself on the bench next to my mom, hoping he would walk by.

Finally, after what felt like an interminable wait, Ray strolled nonchalantly up to the bench. "What's up?" he said way too casually, hands plunged in his pockets.

I was overwhelmed with a poker-hot ferocity. I lost it, right there in the middle of the square. He hadn't done anything wrong, not really. But all those years of practised, professional verbal duelling, the scorched insults traded back and forth between us — they were lying in wait inside me, and now they had a place to go.

I screamed, "Where the hell did you go? We've been waiting for you!"

He rolled his eyes, shook his head. I remember reading somewhere that a relationship is over when eye-rolling becomes the main form of communication.

I started to whip out all the ancient attacks I'd been inflicting upon him ever since he was young. Not surprisingly, he was up for the challenge. Because we were both angry, not at each other, but at this goddamned cancer eating away at our mother. We dug out all the old insults, the tried and true ones: you thoughtless, selfish bastard (me); you sanctimonious bitch, you think you're better than everyone else just because you're a professor (him). We added some new creative ones to the batch, too: don't think you're so great just because you finally got off your ass and came over here from Vancouver, now that you have a son and partner, you're too good for us, huh? (him). And from me, this whopper: you only came on this trip to get compassionate leave from work — that one, in hindsight, so cruel that even now I cringe at ever having dared say it out loud, let alone thought it.

Our fight was one for the ages, it was that good.

As we traded these fiery barbs, my mom just sat there, slumped, on the bench. She had witnessed and intervened in many of these fights in the past. I remember one when we were kids that left a small scar on my face, his fingers scratching me at the side of my eye (my fault, not his; it's hard for me to admit I asked for that one — I'd dared him to scratch me). I'd milked that one for all it was worth, telling everyone I knew that my brother had hit me. I remember my mother's pained look when she witnessed that fight so many years ago, and now I wondered how it must feel to see this one, this explosion of anger, while she was hurting. This time she was too exhausted to try to stop it.

We fenced each other with our tropes, weaponized the stories we believed and didn't believe about each other. The crowds mostly ignored us, the two Brown people screaming in the square. Children raced around us, continuing to play as if nothing was wrong. As the insults fell from our mouths, I could almost see them floating like scorching embers into the blindingly blue sky. I hoped the clouds would swallow them whole. I suddenly felt nauseous and dropped to the ground. My knees hit the cold cobblestones. I was breathing heavily, and my head was spinning.

I was not sick physically. I knew I wasn't. But I was burning up with anger, brimming with fury, wanting to lash out even more. I was nowhere near done, nowhere near it. There was nowhere else for my pain to go.

Ray looked at me weeping on the pavement and reached out a hand to lift me up. He was panting from our exchange. A child rushed by, jostling me. I glanced at our mother. She was in pain, I could see, not only from her tongue but from what we had inflicted upon her. It wouldn't be the last time my brother and I exchanged barbs, but it would be the last time we did so with so such bitterness.

My brother took her arm, and we slowly wended our way out of the square, my mother clutching the train to her heart as if it were a prized jewel.

Such awfulness in a beautiful place, I thought, as the snowflakes fell in picture-perfect prettiness around us. *Such awfulness in such a beautiful place.*

Speech Patterns

Another question for you:

Do you ever think about how you speak?

Like, really think about it?

We were on Innisfil Beach, maybe in 2000, my mother, her best friend Zarah and I. Her friend was visiting from Virginia and longed to see the beach. I was tasked with driving them there. I was resentful because I had been forced to take the day off work to play chauffeur.

But once there, my disposition changed. I closed my eyes, enjoying the gentle blizzard of wind and sand and salt that flitted about my face, listening to the caws of the seagulls. My mom's laughter, like gemstones, cut through the sound of the waves. I was slowly unwinding, allowing the anger to dissipate.

"So warm, the water!" Mom cried out from the shore. Her voice only just registering over the sound of the waves.

Zarah looked at me, screwed up her nose as if she had smelled something odd. "Fari has always done that."

"Done what?" I said, my eyes wandering. I wasn't paying attention — I was watching a gorgeous golden retriever fetch a red ball on the white-white sand that only Innisfil offers.

"Messes up how she speaks — switches the subject and predicate around. Notice she doesn't say, 'The water is warm.' She'll describe it and then tell you what she's describing. You've never noticed?"

I shook my head. Nope. Never.

But then I started to notice. *So blue, the sky! So white, the snow! So beautiful, your son.*

I always thought Zarah was a little jealous of my mom. She wasn't the only one. When I was six, a childhood friend told me his mother told him, with what I'm guessing was not a little scorn, that my mom looked like she ironed her jeans. This made no sense to me at the time — only later would I see how insulting it was. This lazy cruelty passed on from mother to son to me.

Was Zarah implying something about my mother's English? Her impeccable, perfect English? The endless volumes of Shakespeare she'd imposed upon me . . . The clarity of her writing in her early journals . . . How dare Zarah, my mom's oldest friend, the woman she called her sister, speak this way about her?

But why switch these, predicate and subject? I see now why she did it. It was her boundless hunger for what she loved, her endless enthusiasm for it, that overwhelmed the subject. Her delight in the moment caught her off guard, so much so that it engulfed the grammar of the sentence, her words tumbling out before she could catch herself.

So maybe this is why I'm not surprised when I hear Cole saying, years later, just as he's beginning to speak, "Mama, so big, the tree!"

I wonder where he's learned this. I don't do it. I ask Bruce if I do. He says no.

I reach out to correct him, to say, *No, Cole, it's actually "The tree is so big"* . . . and then I stop myself.

Yes, Cole. That's right. So big, the tree. So big.

Frankfurt–Zurich–Miami

When I left Frankfurt, it was Christmas Eve, 2015. My mother and brother were also at the airport. It turned out that Infusio closed down for the holidays between December 22 and January 5, which left my brother and mother with no place to go. Funny that — why we weren't told this before we arrived was a mystery to me. We floundered around trying to find a place for them to stay, but it was Christmastime and hotels were booked up. My mother and brother decided to do something daring. They made plans to go to a holiday resort in Malta.

I was of the belief that this trip to Malta would be difficult for my mom, given that she struggled to walk, but she was convinced she could do it and I could see she wanted my brother to have a happy holiday *somewhere*. We were fortunate that Ray's best friend, Allan, flew from Toronto to help with my mother's care and keep my brother company. I'll always be grateful to him for that.

The story about Malta is not mine to tell. I was not there.

I felt guilty for going to see my son and partner in Miami during this time. Looking at the faces of the other family members at the clinic before it closed for the holidays had started to break something in me. We all shared the same look of desperate despair. The other clients at Infusio had varied ailments — ranging from Lyme disease to lupus to cancer, the clinic's speciality — but when some of them told me this was their second or third visit, and they weren't getting better, I began for the first time to wonder about the clinic's efficacy. This growing uncertainty made me feel even worse about leaving. But as my brother alluded to darkly, "You will have to come back again, Minelle . . . To do more heavy lifting."

I flew to Zurich on my way to Miami, and on that first flight, my pain really barged in, like a loud-mouthed uninvited guest at my front door. The shingles made themselves known to me in a new way, greeting me with unabashed glee, the neurological symptoms coming on so hard this time that I could hardly hold my beloved Sheaffer fountain pen as I tried to scrawl my feelings out on paper to distract myself. The flight attendants generously plied me with frosty ice packs and foreign pills I didn't recognize, but nothing helped. The tears came freely, and I was not sure if I was crying from the pain of the shingles or of leaving my mother behind in Europe.

In my journal from that trip, I have to squint to make sense of my handwriting. It is all in large loops, the writing spidery, shaky. On some pages, a melodramatic "I am in pain!" in big letters that take up an entire piece of paper. On others, a microscopic scrawl in the corner, "Please God, help me."

When I flew from Zurich to Miami, though, my prayers were answered and the pain momentarily subsided. Maybe it was something about being over the Atlantic again. The healing power of the ocean. My friend Sonja might tell me that the oceans remember us. When I disembarked from the plane and saw my little boy for the first time in almost a month, he quickly peeled away from his dad and gleefully called out "Mama!" He ran at me at a furious pace, flinging himself into my arms in the crowded airport.

Feeling his sturdy, healthy three-year-old body in my arms made me believe in God again. His candy-apple breath and his singsong voice lulled me into temporarily forgetting, but only just for a moment, the agony my mother must have been in.

Jerry

Years before my experience with Zarah on the beach, when I was in grade ten, someone else had questioned my mother's voice.

I'd been admitted into a class where you could study whatever you wanted for a few periods each day. Our progress was hard to evaluate, so the teacher invited parents to come in to speak with him. He was a long-haired American hippie with a curly, wiry auburn beard, sparkling eyes and a deep voice. He encouraged all of his students to read *Zen and the Art of Motorcycle Maintenance*. I held a vague suspicion that he smoked pot on his own time. He always seemed eerily calm.

My mom went to the meeting. "*Mashallah, junam*. He was pleased with your work!"

The next day, when I walked into the classroom, Jerry, as he encouraged us to call him, gestured to me, patted the empty chair next to him. "You didn't tell me your mother has an accent," he said.

I frowned. "No, she doesn't."

He cocked his head. "Um, yes, she does. An Indian accent."

"No. She doesn't have an accent at all."

He raised his eyebrows and shrugged. *Whatever.* I walked away feeling flummoxed. I played my mom's voice over and over in my head. No. Nothing. No accent at all. My dad's voice, yes. Indian accent. I'd even imitated it for white friends, as a joke, at French immersion summer camp, speaking French with an Indian accent. Thinking about that now has me burning with shame.

But my mom? No. I couldn't hear it.

Maenam

I'm out with Bruce on a Saturday night. I'm wearing a new clingy black dress. I even have a little makeup on for a change. I'm flushed from a glass of rosé and am balanced precariously on a stool in a fancy Thai restaurant on 4th Avenue in Vancouver. I'm telling him about this experience in high school. He smiles at me, tells me he always remembers my mom having had an accent — he noticed it from day one.

I am stubborn with him, saying, "No, no accent." I confess to him about imitating my dad.

He asks me if maybe I'd been imitating my mom, not my dad, and I just didn't know it.

Burmese Food for Chanukah

With my mom on my mind, I dug my toes into the toasty crystalline sand on a beach in Lake Worth, Florida. I wondered how she was doing that day in Malta and scratched my shoulder mindlessly. The fury-filled pustules had mercifully died down, but the nerve pain persisted. I felt torn between drinking in the sunshine on my face and feeling guilty for enjoying the sand and surf and the pungent scent of brine in the air. But Ray called daily to tell me that she was dutifully taking her medicine. He kept assuring me there was nothing I could do. *Just enjoy yourself, Minelle*, he would say. So, I valiantly tried to enjoy my holiday with my little boy as he giggled and played in the cresting waves.

"Minelle, honey — there's whitefish in the fridge. You can have it with some bialys. I got them just for you!" Bruce's mother said when I got home.

"No, thank you, Roz. I'm not hungry."

She didn't realize I caught the look she gave my husband. *When is she going to eat?*

Although my appetite had abandoned me, I kept thinking about the meals my mom used to make for me when I was a kid. I think I knew then that I would never experience them in quite the same way again. In the darkness of my anticipatory grief, I was already beginning to mourn the tastes of my childhood. Of course, the dish I missed the most was *khao-swe*.

I kept thinking about that dish. While we watched the Kennedy Center Honors on PBS — a ritual in that house — I spontaneously declared that I was going to make *khao-swe* for everyone for a belated Chanukah dinner. Bruce said nothing, knowing better than to arrest this sudden burst of life from me.

I drove Bruce's mother's Prius to Whole Foods the next day to pick up the necessary ingredients: egg noodles, chicken, chilies. I improvised around the lack of gram flour and fish sauce at the store. I looked up myriad recipes for *khao-swe* on the web, but none seemed right. And I knew, even before I turned on the stove to boil the water, that I would get it wrong.

The extended family arrived just as I put the finishing touches on the meal. I put out a lot of small bowls filled with garnishes: sour lemon quarters; sliced hard-boiled eggs, the yolks bright orange; diced spring onions; chopped cilantro. Don't forget the dried red chili peppers! And then the pièce de résistance: a big bowl of *khao-swe* curry, piping hot, with wafts of steam curling seductively around it.

My fear: would this fly with Bruce's Jewish family? This family for whom a celebratory dinner typically meant beef brisket, challah, matzo ball soup, smoked salmon? What was I doing, being so bold as to share my beloved family meal with them for Chanukah? I felt vulnerable, stupid, even childish. I hid for a minute behind the refrigerator door. *Idiot*, I chastised myself. I took a chunk out of the whitefish container with my finger and plunked it in my mouth, hoping no one was looking.

"Minelle, what do I do with this?" someone called out from the dining room.

I rushed out and explained how to prepare the dish. They obediently followed. I watched as they tentatively added the bits and pieces to their plates. They ladled the hot curry on top of their noodles, maybe a little tentatively but not without care.

And . . . everyone liked it! Some even enthused over it. But the ones who really, really loved it were the ones who'd married into Bruce's family. Bruce's cousin's Chinese American wife, Carolina, went in for second helpings. I'd fallen in love with her as soon as we'd met a few years earlier; she is a state judge whom I felt a deep affection for when we started talking about race right off the bat. Our conversations since then were always peppered with laughter, mutual recognition — no small talk here. I quietly schemed family trips to Olympia, Washington, to spend more time with her. She didn't say much about the *khao-swe*, but she gave me a look — she knew what I was up to. She knew this was about more than just food.

There were no leftovers.

I jubilantly carried the dirty bowls back to the sink to be washed, feeling my mom's presence as the din of laughter encased us.

Another family satisfied by dinner — not necessarily the family I had ever anticipated or dared to hope for, to love.

The Ambulance Ride

My mom and brother returned to Toronto on January 19, 2016. I had been back at Roundhouse for a few weeks, going through the motions as if in a daze. On the phone from Toronto, my brother sounded truly dejected for the first time. It was clear that the treatment in Frankfurt had not worked. No one admitted it outright, but it was obvious. The last words I remember hearing from the dazzlingly handsome and perfectly coiffed specialist at Infusio were "When she goes, it will be quick."

That was all that the clinic offered us in the end. It did give us hope. I remember finding some macabre comfort in that, knowing that she would not be in pain for too much longer.

Years later, I would search the clinic online again and discover myriad reviews from dissatisfied clients.

I flew back to Toronto from Vancouver as quickly as possible to be by her side. When I arrived at her front door in Markham, I plunked down my bag, took one long, weary look at her and saw from her sallow face and agonized eyes just how much pain she was in. It was the first time I had ever come home and not heard her voice ringing happily in the hallway or her smile falling upon me when she could no longer speak.

When Ray solemnly told me that she was no longer getting out of bed to say her Namaz, I knew that things were dire. Some rituals are more than routine. Some rituals are lifeblood, sustenance, a quiet request for repair. I called her family doctor, who had almost become a family friend. I begged her to come around, but she refused. I sputtered something about how my mom had been her patient for twenty years and how dare she refuse this one request. I slammed down the phone. When she came to the hospital later to pay her respects, I didn't make eye contact with her. Ray said I was being childish; I didn't care.

I realized I had no recourse. I reluctantly called 911, my fingers trembling. Within minutes, I could hear the siren bleating down the street. I tried to make space for the EMTs when they rushed in, brushed the many bottles of painkillers from the coffee table to the floor as they gently placed my mother on a stretcher to take her to the hospital.

During the ambulance ride, she smiled at me, exhausted. I don't need to tell you I held her hand.

At the hospital, I began the seemingly endless process of advocating for her. It's what we all do, of course: speak for our loved ones who are ill, fight for their right to health care. I wanted them to have the whole story because she could no longer tell it.

The triage specialists immediately recognized that she was beyond what they could offer in the ER and ushered her into palliative care.

Palliative — the only word scarier than *cancer* to me.

Palliative — a word that coarsely means taking care of the symptoms, rather than seeking a cure.

Nirmal Hriday

While she was in palliative, I kept thinking about my sixteenth summer.

Grade eleven. I regularly blared Whitney Houston's "I Wanna Dance with Somebody" on my stereo and danced madly around my room, singing along at the top of my lungs. I was in love with Richard, the seventeen-year-old tennis pro who worked at the community tennis clubhouse. I wrote him long, plaintive letters with my cheap but cherished Sheaffer fountain pen, impassioned letters I would never dare send him, of course. He had no idea I was alive. We all know that story. We have all lived that story at one point or another. But that is not the point of this particular tale.

This is the point.

I only cared about three things: Richard, my pastel-pink Naf Naf outfits and my music (Whitney Houston, the Police and other much more cringey eighties bands that might make you squirm if I told you). Nothing else. I had perfected the art of the squint, the eye roll, the huff and sigh that mothers all over the world are privy to from their teenaged daughters. And my mother? She had had enough.

Over dinner one evening she casually announced, "Minelle and I are going to Kolkata this summer."

I looked up from my biryani, pushed aside my plate. "No, we are not," I said. *There's no way.* Richard would be in the clubhouse every day, and I was not about to miss that.

But it turned out we were going. I prevaricated and then thought, *Fine, we can go shopping and get clothes made and . . .*

Then she said, "We are going to work with Mother Teresa and the Missionaries of Charity."

With who? With what?

Apparently, my mother had written a letter to the Missionaries of Charity suggesting that we volunteer at their orphanage for two weeks. As a Montessori teacher, my mother was convinced she could work with the children, and she wanted to bring me along. The nuns wrote back on brown onion skin paper, protesting that I was too young to volunteer. But my mother was adamant. She made a case for my so-called maturity, and they reluctantly agreed.

"We are going. And that, *junam*, is *that.*"

I dreaded the trip in the months before we left. I was sullen on the plane all the way across the oceans. But when we arrived, I was surprised. The India I knew in Mumbai was entirely different to the one in Kolkata. My father's family was not there. This was my mother's India, and she wanted me to see it with her. But more than that, she wanted me to lose my stubborn, arrogant teenage pride that made me disdainful of everyone, but mostly her. My uncouth white way of being would be eradicated by the time we went home — *inshallah.*

Every morning in my mother's India, I found myself lying on my stomach on the stone-cold linoleum floor of the orphanage to be closer to the young girls — because they were all young girls, of course; no boys in the orphanage, boys were prized, girls were shunned — colouring with broken Crayola crayons in the colouring books we'd brought them. I spoke no Bengali so we learned to speak through songs and shared laughter.

Do you want this burnt sienna crayon, this periwinkle blue?

Yes, ji, *Minelle*, they giggled.

The sunshine on the girls' faces when my mother and I arrived at the orphanage every morning was like waking up to a glorious shimmering day. I sometimes saw the nuns watching me with the girls, playing catch, making funny faces, my metallic braces prominently on display, before they turned to my mother and smiled serenely.

My sullenness dulled and then dissipated.

One afternoon, my mother told me that we would not go to the orphanage; she had arranged for us to go someplace altogether new. She said this place was called Nirmal Hriday — loosely translated to the Centre for the Dead and Dying. I didn't want to go. Why would I want to go?

When we got there, I was asked by the attendant to offer an elderly woman some water. I grabbed a cloudy glass and walked over to her. She was lying in a cot, almost lifeless. She looked up at me, yellow-eyed. The nun motioned to me to take her in my arms. When I did, I discovered she was paper-thin, weightless, a feather floating to the ground. She had a milk-bottle pallor; I saw the blue in her bones. Her eyes pleaded with me. I offered her the water, and she coughed it down with each heavy swallow. After finishing the water, she collapsed in my arms, evidently exhausted by the mere act of drinking. Years later, I would think of her when my mother slumped in my arms as I tried to get her to drink.

My mother was tending to another patient. "Mom," I whispered hoarsely. "Ask the nun how old this lady is." I imagined the woman in my arms as my grandmother, great-grandmother. The years she must have seen, the children she may have borne, the onerousness of her obstacles.

My mom turned to the nun, who quietly said something back to her. My mom smiled faintly at me, a sad, sweet smile, and with care whispered, "Muni, she's sixteen. She's your age."

I was shocked. I didn't know what to say. This girl would never know the joys of a racket in her hand as she made a clean volley, the pleasure of a shared giggle with girlfriends, the solid feel of a silver fountain pen scratching out a love letter to a crush. I stroked the girl's hair gently, said a small prayer. When she fell asleep in my arms, I slowly extricated myself from her embrace.

When we left, I found I could not speak. But I didn't need to say anything, and my mom knew that too.

That night, I headed up to the rooftop of the apartment we were staying in. It was sunset, the view reminding me of the vibrant colours of the broken crayons back at the orphanage: vivid tangerine, antique brass, pink sherbet. The roosters crowed. I heard the horns of noisy rickshaws and the barks of stray mutts through the smoky orange haze. Somewhere, off in the distance, I heard a song from a tinny radio. It was "I Wanna Dance with Somebody." I would never hear that song again without thinking about that day, the song holding an entirely different meaning for me because of where I heard it, and how the geography resonates for me now. Every story, always another story.

The trip — working with the orphans — was a form of white-adjacent "voluntourism" to be sure, though I wouldn't see it that way until many years later. It was also a chance for my mother to show me her old haunts, and for me to witness her childlike enthusiasm for places she adored.

And when I returned home, I wrote about my experience with that beloved fountain pen of mine. I shared it with my father, who said he knew someone at the *Toronto Star* who might want to read it. Six months later, on Christmas Day, the piece came out, a front-page story above the fold in the Insight section. There were photos of me with the kids standing behind me, grinning. And my father handed me a cheque. I still remember how much it was for.

"No, Dad! You keep it," I said. "You take the money."

"But why, Muni?"

All I could think of was Jo in *Little Women*, who handed her father her very first writing cheque. I wanted the money to go back to our family, I explained. My first writing job and my first foray into journalism. My mother witnessed this exchange in our hallway, the same hallway where I'd hit my head years earlier. She smiled proudly in the background, then winked at me. I smiled back. Nothing else needed to be said.

The opposite of palliative.

White Bedsheets in Palliative Care

Like at Infusio, the palliative ward at Markham Stouffville Hospital was all about whiteness. I became obsessed with the crisp white bedsheets. I would sneak into the storage cupboards to admire them. They were scratchy from years of bleach and smelled vaguely antiseptic, but they were always perfectly folded, one on top of the other. Mine at home were always dishevelled, un-ironed. I could never fold them so beautifully. These were impeccable but old. After all, they had seen a lot, these sheets.

The nurses came in and changed my mother's sheets regularly — the snap of the sheets as they made the bed was the very sound of efficiency. The pallor of my mother's skin matched the colour of the sheets. The nurses kindly offered me an extra set for the white leather chair that leaned back but only barely.

I would end up spending two weeks sleeping on that hard, cold, uncomfortable chair.

I became friends with the folks who came in to visit their parents or grandparents in the wing. I felt like a barfly at her local. I could tell who had come in recently and who had been visiting for a long time just from the looks on their faces. Palliative care was like a snapshot of leaden public intimacy. At night, I padded around the floor in my polka-dotted Joe Fresh pyjamas. It was deathly quiet except for the constant hum of the life-support machines.

Every day my phone rang from Vancouver.

Mama, are you coming home soon?
No, junam, *not for a few weeks, I don't think.*
But can we come see you soon, then?
Maybe, junam, *maybe.*

Relatives dropped by, peered around the curtain to pay their respects. If I was lucky, they would drop off *hinjo*, a vermicelli fish soup my mother adored. Or, if I was really lucky, they would bring steaming containers of *tahdig* and *chelo kabab*. It would get cold while they visited, and so after they left, I would reheat the food in the common-room microwave. The TV would always be on in there, some ancient sitcom blaring, the laugh track loud. There would always be a bottle of New Zealand Sauvignon Blanc that I'd stashed away on the bottom shelf of the communal refrigerator, chilling.

These are the happy stories. Do they sound happy? I don't know. I wouldn't have thought there could be happy stories in palliative, but here they are. I think of the time the stranger who had flown in from British Columbia to be with her stepmother noticed I was practically living at the hospital and the next day handed me a gift bag that included tube socks from Victoria's Secret and — the best part — a beautiful purple-and-white-paisley fleece blanket.

"I noticed you're staying here every night, and I didn't want you to get cold."

I was overwhelmed with gratitude to this stranger, this woman who offered me something small, but so big. At night, accompanied only by the voices of those machines, I pulled the blanket up close to my chin and listened to my mom's laborious breathing, the breathing specific to those who are about to die. I hope you never know that sound.

I still have that blanket. I use it almost every night. Shelter and memory. In palliative, I would carefully lay it on top of my mother some evenings. I wanted her skin to feel how soft it was. My mother and I both instinctively touched things to understand more about them. When we went shopping, we would walk along the aisles of clothing, picking up material, placing it between thumb and forefinger, experiencing the sensations of the velvet, cashmere, cotton. When she took me on walks as a child, she would encourage me to pick up fallen leaves, saying, "Don't pluck the leaves off the plants, Muni — just feel the leaves on the ground." Don't take the life from them, Muni.

Blanket

And now I want to tell you a little story about another blanket.
Every Nowruz during *sofreh*, my mother would take out a small
green chapbook. The pages are now soft and velvety from use. In it
was this story: Mohammed invited his entire family to meet with
him under a blanket. They gathered, and the angels of mercy circled
around them, asking them to forgive their sins.

"As the Angel Jibreel took a place under the blanket, he said:
'Allah sends this revelation to you: verily, Allah so desires to remove
all impurities from you, O People of the House (Ahlul-Bayt) and
purify you with a perfect purification.'"

We all sat solemnly listening to this story, once a year. I imagined Mohammed's entire family under the blanket, under the sheet,
as we gathered around the table — a family listening to another
family. I always thought of it, too, when I huddled with my parents
and Ray in our den late at night, watching television.

And now, every spring, I read the story out loud to Bruce
and Cole.

Every story, always two stories, or three.

Namaz

"Mama, why do we say prayers?"

"Because they are important."

"Why, Mama, why?"

"Because, they are, just because!" (exasperated)

"But, Mama, I don't understand!"

(I don't understand either, *beti*.) "They matter, they just do!" (big sigh)

They matter because she said them and now we do too. Every night. Clockwork. Ritual. Because it ties her to us.

Rotating Hosts

While I was in the hospital with my mother, I didn't think about *Sense of Place* all that much, to be honest. When my mom was first diagnosed, the interviews provided a brief respite: the energy it took to craft a good question required my full attention and served to distract me. But in palliative, I had no escape any longer. The question on my mind when it came to my mother was not if, but when.

Back on the West Coast, the show went on. Don brought in a wide array of people to host for me while I was away. Occasionally, when I remembered and had time to listen, I tuned in to the show online from my mother's hospital room. I tried not to feel jealous. Freddie, one of the replacement hosts, was exuberant, loud, carefree and nothing like the voice I would have expected to take over my show.

"Aaaand today on *Sense of Place*! We're doing a segment on what you plan to do for Family Day this year! Taking the kids skiing? Or maybe you and the honey have a private getaway planned! Let us know by calling . . ."

Since when had *Sense of Place* become a call-in show?

I walked out of my mom's hospital room and called Don.

"Does Freddie get what we're trying to do with the show? It sounds off," I whispered, trying not to bother the patients.

Don took a beat and said, "Freddie doesn't like what you're doing with the show. It just feels wrong to him."

I winced. I could hear a patient in the room next to me coughing. "Um, he gets that the show is for and by people of colour, right?"

That's when Don said, "He gets it. He just doesn't like it."

Before I'd left for Toronto, I'd tried to bring Freddie up to speed, to delicately explain to him the format and framing of the show. But I could see from his expression that he was stymied — as if my aspirations for the program were truly incomprehensible.

Don went on. "It's not just Freddie who feels that way. Chuck shares Freddie's point of view regarding the content and focus. Look . . . this conversation will have to wait until you get back into town. It would be good to have a more . . . heartfelt conversation in person . . . with more points of view."

I put the phone down and went back in to see my mother. It was clear that if I wasn't there, the show would no longer be my show, even though I had created it. I had enough to hold on to here in the hospital. I would have to let this other thing go, at least for now. I couldn't have them both.

Take Me Home

About two weeks into our stay in palliative, my mother's breathing became even more shallow and jagged. Her eyelids fluttered. The doctor told me that it was typical for a patient to be in palliative around two weeks. I didn't need to ask what happened after that.

I was told to make the calls.

The requisite revolving parade of guests came in to utter their goodbyes. I could see her thin puddle of a body underneath the white bedsheets, that white chair pulled up next to her bedside, hear the whispers uttered. When certain people came in, I knew enough to pull the heavy hospital door shut tight, to give my mom and the guest their privacy. My uncle, her only living sibling, flew in from Auckland, his face grim. I left them alone but could hear him quietly speaking to her. It was not for me to know what was shared between them.

My mom's students came in, one by one. They were a motley crew. I'd learned this, too, as a professor: there's no discernable pattern to the students whose lives we influence, and we can never really guess who'll be moved enough to stay in touch, to reach out. One of my mom's former students in her twenties — admittedly one of my mom's favourites, and mine, too — came in toting a goldfish, the water sloshing around haphazardly in the bowl. "Your mother always liked goldfish," she said, a big grin on her face.

I was surprised. The student didn't know the significance of the goldfish to my mother. But I did. For Nowruz, the Iranian New Year, live goldfish are added to the *haft-seen*, a kind of ceremonial table, as a way of signalling good fortune. But environmentalists and animal-rights activists have urged Iranians to stop practising this perennial rite. I mulled over what I would do with the fish in the after. After Nowruz, goldfish are supposed to be freed into rivers and ponds, but this is almost certain to kill them. I tried hard not to think about the after.

The student's voice dropped down an octave. "That fish — that's for your mom. But this — this is for you." She rummaged around in her battered but fashionable leather purse, looked around to make sure no one was watching like a spy in a comedy, and pulled out a small Ziploc bag. Inside were four blue cylindrical pills.

"Trust me — this will make you feel much better."

I took them out, cradled them in my hand like jewels. Lorazepam.

"The drug of choice in these situations," she said. "It'll knock you right out, and you'll be able to sleep."

It was the first real laugh I'd had in weeks. I marvelled at her ability to shatter the solemnity of the situation. I heaved with gratitude.

It was these small gestures I would come to treasure later. We all have them, of course: vague memories of tumultuous times and of all the people you think will come during the just-before time but who never show. That anger never dissipates. But you remember all the people you never expected to turn up but who do. An estranged friend who comes, and when you see her, you burst into tears. The Islamic studies professor who barely knows you but shows up with a pile of meals in a Longo's shopping bag, including *hinjo* and — yes! — more *chelo kabab*.

Phil, one of my colleagues from my old life at the University of Toronto, wanted to come by, but he was teaching. His mother came in his stead. She entered the ward slightly stooped over, an elderly Greek woman, hands grasping large greasy paper bags full of spanakopita and chicken shawarma still warm in their battered Tupperware containers. I remember a conversation Phil and I had at U of T once — a brief chat that had happened by chance when we passed each other in the hallway — about how he grieved for his dad when he died. He must have remembered.

Phil's mother shuffled around the hospital floor with me a few times, clutching my arm, not saying much. She looked at me in a way that made me feel nested, cared for. It was the look my mom would have given my colleague if she were able.

My mother scribbled on a piece of paper: "Tell Ray to bring by a box of Ferrero Rocher chocolates."

I asked, "Why?"

She wrote back, "To offer people when they come to visit."

Even though she couldn't eat, she wanted to make sure she created an environment of hospitality.

Apart from the procession of guests who came in, one after another like a revolving door, I was alone with my mother. At night, I squeezed beside her in the narrow hospital bed, placing oversized headphones on her ears so she could listen to the song she sang so often to others — the children at her school, her beloved younger brother when he was a child. Maybe you know it. One of the nurses I loved at the hospital — and I loved so many of them for their distinctive personalities and styles of care — had a beautiful singing voice. I timidly asked her if she knew the song, and if she did, if she could sing it for my mom. She was renowned on the ward for her voice. You could hear it echoing down the hallways, if you were lucky.

I recorded her rendition on my cellphone and then placed the headphones on my mother's ears for her to hear.

All things bright and beautiful
All creatures great and small
All things wise and wonderful

'Twas God that made them all
Each little flower that opens
Each little bird that sings
He made their glowing colours
And made their tiny wings
All things bright and beautiful
All creatures great and small
All things wise and wonderful
'Twas God that made them all . . .

My mother must have learned the song during her days in Catholic school. *The ability to hear is the last sense to go*, I remember someone told me once.

I would learn later that this song is a common Christian funeral hymn.

I curled up with my mom on the bed, the purple paisley blanket surrounding us both, and tried to comfort her, her body not moving, but her breathing so loud and languorous. Can the voice have a body? A body that burns with pain? I was slowly running out of questions, questions and time. This was the only one I had left. Well, almost the only one. You know what the last question is.

Around eight the next morning, I gingerly moved from the bed and over to the chair. I didn't want to wake her up. Her breathing was still so laboured. I could see my phone was blowing up; I was receiving texts from my mom's accountant. I picked up the phone to call him and was soon speaking with him in the language of numbers, invoices, paycheques — my mind shifting from her to him. It was then that I heard a new silence enter the room. The sounds of her breathing gone.

I stuttered to my mom's accountant that I had to go and dropped the phone to the ground. I walked over to the bed, placed a finger under her nose. No breath.

At that precise moment, I was relieved. And then I laughed. I laughed. I started laughing manically, even raucously, all by myself, the room still dark, shades still drawn, her body still there but now growing cold. The thought suddenly came to me: *She wanted me away from her when she died. Not anywhere near her, not by her side. Her death was her own.* And how she'd given me a gift, even at the end — making sure I wasn't embracing her as she drew her last painful breath.

I remember laughing, laughing, and I remember being horrified and relieved that I was laughing. I couldn't stop, and I didn't want to stop. I laughed and laughed until I couldn't laugh any more. When I did stop, I was breathing so heavily, I felt winded. Breathing as loudly as she had been before she wasn't.

It was during the next few minutes that I contemplated the arduous process ahead of me — the process of calling everyone. That endless cycle of phone calls, the exaggerated sighs on the phone, the mindless refrain of "Minelle, I'm so sorry" that I was dreading.

So I put it off. I just stopped.

I opened up my laptop and pressed play on Phil Collins's "Take Me Home." If you're of my generation, you probably know this song. Why I chose this stupid song I still don't know. There was something almost ghoulish about this gesture — about me putting it on like I was a defiant teenager, laughing with her about her decision to leave just as I'd left her bedside, returning the favour with my own little joke.

I sat by her bed and listened to the music. I uttered the Muslim prayer we say when someone dies. If you don't know it, I hope you will look it up. It is beautiful. And I didn't call anyone, except the nurse, who came in and checked her pulse and nodded at me sadly, saying, "Yes, you're right. Just take your time."

And I did.

At nine o'clock, an hour later, I called my brother. I knew he needed to sleep. Why burden him at eight a.m. when I knew this day was going to be so long, maybe the longest of his life? The phone rang once, twice, three times, and I hated that I had to make the call he'd made to me in Vancouver all those years ago, to tell me our dad had died. Rotations, again.

When he picked up, he knew. I didn't have to say anything.

I didn't call Bruce. Bruce was there with Ray, at my mother's house. I knew Ray would tell Bruce. And I knew Bruce would tell Cole. The broken telephone of the death notification. They'd flown out a few days ago; we'd known this was coming soon.

My oldest friend in Toronto was my next call. I had known Joylyn since I was two and a half. She was like a cherished sister. When I reached her, she just asked me a question. She asked, "You want me to come?" And I said, "Yes." She came, even though she hadn't driven her car in months on the highway after a serious concussion — she still came. Because that is who she is. And when she arrived, she laughed at the surreal scene: the laptop playing Phil Collins on repeat and me clad in sturdy ugly Nike runners and jeans, a look that we both despise. She laughed at me and I laughed with her, in that small dark little room.

Before my brother turned up, I took a long look at my mother's lifeless body, a little bird, feathers crumpled, withered and weary. I will spare you all the details of what a dead body looks like because if you know you know, and if you don't, I don't want you to know yet, not really.

But what I wish I had known was to take off her rings earlier.

My mother wore three rings. The first was a ruby surrounded by diamonds. The second was a rusty-orange glass ring worth pennies that her mosque gave out sometimes to offer solace and ease. And the third was a ring I had bought her while I was a postdoctoral fellow travelling in Sydney, Australia, and feeling a little flush for the first time in my life. A token of my affection, it was a thin gold band with a miniature opal in it, veined with thin rainbows. It cost me maybe two hundred dollars, and I always regretted not spending more because she never took that thing off. She loved it.

And on the day she died, I tried to take off all the rings and couldn't.

I pulled, tugged, tried soap and water — and felt like a fool pulling on my mother's wrinkled, mottled fingers.

Finally a nurse came in and noticed what I was doing. She smiled knowingly — these gentle souls who have seen everything — and disappeared for a mere minute, then came back with a spool of thread.

"Tie this around her finger, just above her knuckle. The rings will slide off."

It felt odd, wrapping her fingers in blue thread, watching the blood that was no longer circulating gather in pools above her knuckles. The rings slid neatly off, a magic trick without the usual accompanying joy.

Remember the Goldfish?

In case you were wondering:

The fish died the day after she did. I found its sad, bloated body floating belly up in the murky water. I didn't have to take it to the nearby Toogood Pond to try to give it a second life as I'd meant to do. It was gone already.

Bed Bath & Beyond

My first trip outside the hospital, I told my brother to drive me to
Bed Bath & Beyond so I could buy him a blanket similar to the one
the stranger had given me in palliative care. I knew he didn't need
one, but I want him to have something soft and cozy after I left.
I found one almost identical to mine.

He took it warily. "Minelle, I really don't need this."

"Take it, Ray, take it," I insisted.

"Minelle, I really don't need it."

Anne Michaels: "I see that I must give what I most need."

May It Have a Happy Ending

When I returned to her house, the first day in the after, I started rummaging around, and found the usual objects I expected to see: silly souvenirs from my childhood, faded report cards. But what surprised me was the extraordinary number of prayer books. They were everywhere — hidden away in darkened and dusty corners of the house. Under bed pillows even, she must have slept with them. Buried under old scarves in the hall closet. Some small, some large: some Qurans were big maroon bricks; one small, silver, the size of a charm on a bracelet. When I pried the tiny book open, there was a tinier book inside. I would learn later from the internet that this charm was a *taweez*, a talisman of sorts that is worn or hung somewhere to ward off harm and bring in good fortune.

I packed up all the prayer books to take to the mosque later. I refused to be sentimental on this point. But one prayer insisted on fluttering out of her book of *duas* as I was lugging them down the stairs. It was all but six words, scrawled on a slip of paper with "Garden Basket" printed on it. From one of those pads you used to get in the mail sometimes, a promotion for the local grocery store. Back when we all kept pads of paper near our telephones attached to the wall. Maybe you remember.

On it, scrawled in her beautiful handwriting: *Sulaam Moon Kowlum Min R Rabin Rahim*

And under it, the translation: *May it have a happy ending*

What does this mean, this small simple prayer?

I shuffled the words around in my mind and in my mouth, reciting them out loud the way my mother might have done: happy ending, may it have; ending, happy have it may. Whichever way I altered their order, nothing shifted the palpable power of those six words.

Was it happy for you, Mom? Was it okay at the end, beginning, middle? Could this be the prayer for all of us, the hope that all our endings are happy, that even if the beginning is rough-and-tumble, perhaps the ending could be less full of grief, freight, struggle?

I will never know what the ending was like for her, but the morphine injections and the moans told me more than I ever wanted or needed to know.

I read that prayer every night now when I say my Namaz, taking out the tiny scrap of paper, opening it with deep sanctity. It's worn now, and I don't want to lose it, damage it. The hope so deeply haunting in those few words.

You don't want to leave things unfinished. We hear this so much when someone is about to die, you have to sort out the loose ends, you have to say all the things you have to say. But what is this obsession with endings, tidy endings, clean, neat knots? Life is a messy series of unfinished things. We can't be this afraid of unfinished endings.

May It Have a Happy Ending. Because endings are a product we have created — nothing really ends; nothing really ever begins, either. Because whoever decided that beginnings and endings were opposites was wrong. In every ending, a new beginning. And there is no such thing as a happy ending during end times, which it feels like we are all now in, anyway.

I am trying to write for you a happy ending. A happy ending during end times, which is, of course, impossible but also cannot be impossible.

It just can't.

PART FIVE

NUMBERS AND SIGNS

"Sometimes your tongue is removed, sometimes you still it of your own accord. Sometimes you live, sometimes you die. Sometimes you have a name, sometimes you are named for what — not who — you are. The story always looks a little different, depending on who is telling it."

— CARMEN MARIA MACHADO, *In the Dream House*

Her Memorial

The burial, the *jinaaza*, happened right away. Her death on a Wednesday, her burial on Friday. There were many details to be handled, and my phone would not stop ringing. It took my mind off her passing, the brusque business of the burial. I'd been there before, planning a funeral for my dad. Maybe you have been too. This wasn't my first rodeo, and I was brisk and prepared with my death notebook full of dates and figures and to-do lists. It allowed me to forget about her, if only briefly.

Then I began planning her memorial. Ray and I wanted to hold it at her former school, the Montessori school she'd started almost twenty years earlier and which she had fortunately sold in the past year. Years ago, she'd told me that if she hadn't been Muslim and wasn't going to be buried in the Islamic burial plot near Yonge and Sheppard, she would want to be cremated and have her ashes scattered around her school. I think she would have loved to have been nestled up against the big oak tree at the front of the school and around the lush bulrushes at the back, flanking the stream. I couldn't give her the opportunity to forever be in that place she loved, but I could ask to have her memorial at her school. The issue, though, was that her school was no longer hers. We needed permission from the new owners to hold the memorial there.

When I called the husband and asked, he was tentative. But I cajoled him, trying to explain how important this would have been to her. He was nervous, and I could tell he wanted to say yes — he had been in constant contact with my mother while negotiating the deal to purchase her school and had been charmed by her, but this decision was one he'd have to make with his wife.

When he came back on the phone, he said yes, but I had the sense he'd had to fight for it. He told me he hoped the memorial wouldn't be large, and I assured him it would be small - there'd been no time to tell people.

But I was dead wrong. Hundreds of her students, mentors, teachers, friends and family turned up at her beloved school, the place she'd adored so much. So many people, young and old, former students with their toddlers in tow. The place was teaming, filled to the rafters, people spilling out the door. The avalanche of well-wishers undid me.

Tamir, my former graduate student, now beloved friend, quietly set up a screen and sound system so that some of the mourners could go up to the second floor of the school and watch the memorial service from up there.

I hadn't been in the school for more than a year, and there were signs of my mother everywhere — all the little things that made this crumbling old Victorian house a home. The miniature ten-speed bike perched on the fireplace. Framed pictures of some of my brother's and my artwork from when we were kids. The small curios she placed everywhere to make the school a nest of care.

People continued to pour in. I greeted them on the wooden porch, shaking hands, hugging strangers, Cole on my hip. My greasy black hair was in need of cutting; my face was wan.

The new owners, in particular the wife, looked at me with lips tightly pursed. She hissed at me through her teeth, "The fire department will come and close us down!"

Believe it or not, I was grateful to her for this quietly seething outburst. The people-pleaser in me became so wrought with guilt that throughout the service, I forgot to feel sad about my mother. I was too subsumed with worry about this other woman – one ugly guilt replacing another, one much easier to handle than the other.

I whispered to my brother during one touching eulogy: "That woman is scowling at me."

My brother looked at her, and then rolled his eyes, but in a way that said, *We are in this together.* I start to giggle, and not for the first time that day. I tried to cough to stifle my laughter but couldn't. What is this tendency toward laughter in grief? I hadn't expected it, not at all.

Do you want to hear how hard I'd laughed earlier that day? I almost told you, but then I forgot. That's the way grief works, I guess. In the private religious ceremony before the memorial, I'd nearly choked on my laughter sitting cross-legged on the carpeted floor of the mosque. My mother's death ceremony coincided with *Jumma*, noon prayers, and the Mullah spoke eloquently about, of all things, the dangers of addictions – gambling and, in particular, alcohol. So haram! That word that I'd heard my mother utter with such horror and disgust over the years – about dogs, yes, but also whenever she saw my brother pick up a piece of bacon or when she saw me drinking a glass of Sauvignon Blanc.

When the Mullah began to speak about these dangers, I started chuckling uncontrollably, the laughter surging up my throat. I felt unable to stop. I whipped my head around to catch the eye of my smart-ass baby cousin, then in her twenties, who always picks up on everything and yet says so little. When I did, the speed of my movement made my hijab fall over my shoulder. My cousin raised an eyebrow, smirked and gave me the best look – I knew she had my number. We saw each other in this sacred space. I placed my hand over my mouth, trying to mask the sound. But it was hopeless. It was out.

Even in death, she still found a way to preach to me.

The Third Night without Her

The first night I could live without her. The second night as well. The third night felt harder.

After the *jinaaza*, a small group of tight-knit extended family — first cousins, and my brother — piled into my mother's unkempt house. I had called Molly Maid to have them come and clean the place while we were in the hospital, but they didn't seem to pick up every little bit of loose cat litter around the wooden banisters of the stairwell or the dust bunnies that turned up here and there. I wondered how many of her dead skin cells remained in those little grey balls of dirt, and I had the crazy idea to capture them in a resealable plastic bag, place it tenderly under my pillow that night, relish it like a lovely lemon lozenge under my tongue.

My family piled into the house, and I could feel our collective euphoric exhaustion. My relatives sank into the cantaloupe leather couch with relief, just one piece of ugly aged furniture I would have a moving van take away in the next year.

"Let's go get ice cream," my cousin suggested. She was a pro at death. I wish she wasn't, but there it was. She'd spoken at her father's funeral, her mother's, now my mother's. And here, in her knowing, she was offering us the expansive quiet generosity of reprieve.

I turned to Cole who, upon hearing the words *ice cream*, had clapped his hands and shrieked "Yes!" My brother, never one to turn down ice cream, nodded.

Bruce seemed to realize the plan was set in stone now, and we posed the unspoken question to each other without saying a word: who would go with Cole? I shook my head no, not me, and he knew this was not the time to push it. I couldn't stop looking at various items that are hers, that were hers: the porcelain plate with the painted image of a young girl dancing in the rain (meant to go to my cousin, but we couldn't find it after we'd finished packing); the beautiful crystal candelabras, *shamdan* in Farsi, that were meant to be used someday at someone's wedding (maybe mine, if Bruce and I ever chose to get married? Maybe my cousin's?). I told them all to go, get out of the house, I needed some time alone. No, I didn't say that. I only thought it. Instead I said brightly, "Go, have fun!" And as they walked out I could hear them picking out their treats: "I'm getting a Blizzard with Smarties!" "I'm getting a Peanut Buster Parfait!"

I was dimly aware that I was now the matriarch of the family: the oldest in our quartet of four cousins. I wasn't sure what to do with this information. How could I possibly know how to be an elder, that sacred word? I didn't have that kind of wisdom. In the years to come, I would fail all my cousins over and over again, or so I would tell myself. Who would I turn to now for guidance?

I wandered aimlessly around the house, touching things idly that she'd touched merely two weeks earlier. Then minutes — hours? — later, I heard the front door slam and there was a chorus of happy voices echoing through the house. I could hear Cole padding up the stairs, saying, "Mama, I got a choco-cone! Look!" His face was covered in chocolate and his fingers encased in melted vanilla ice cream. One of the dust bunnies slowly drifted from the top banister all the way down to the main floor where my family was still enthusing over their dessert choices. I scooped up my son and buried my face in his neck, marvelling at my family's ability to find joy even in the most macabre of moments.

First Interview in the After

After two weeks of living and sleeping in palliative care and two weeks in the after — weeks filled with the *ghusl* and funeral, with sorting and sealing her beautiful clothes into giant Ziploc bags — I returned to work.

I managed to get to the station without crying. I opened the heavy front glass doors. I dumped my bag and its contents onto my serpentine-shaped desk, and I thought for a second, *It's all going to be okay.* A visitor sticker from the hospital fell out of my bag, and I tried to shove it out of the way without anyone noticing. *I'm fine, really.*

But then I saw Aaron. He looked at me with that particular tight combination of pity and kindness that I now associated with grieving. I wanted to burst into tears, right there in the newsroom. Aaron was intuitive and could sense what was about to happen, so he gestured to the studio — *Want to go in there for a minute?*

I did.

Aaron asked me without words how I was. He'd experienced loss before: a grandparent, a few others too. And with that look, it all came out; I started to tell him what it'd been like. It was the first time I would narrate this story in full, and in time I'd learn how to tell it with greater flourishes, knowing when to stop, start, pause for effect, highlight more important moments to make it more compelling. Those of us who know grief have learned how to tell this story well over time. But at that particular moment, I didn't embellish, I didn't flourish. I just plainly told him what I was feeling.

Kerry came in and chuckled softly. "Can't put you on air like this now, can we?" I could see he was grasping for a joke to make me laugh, but nothing seemed to be coming to mind. He awkwardly patted me on the shoulder. "Good to have you back, kid." Then he saw his moment and lit up like a Christmas tree, that grin of his making me smile in spite of it all. "God, you should have seen Freddie try to take over for you. That was a treat!"

I knew Kerry was pulling out all the stops to try to make me feel better. But it wasn't enough, not quite yet, anyway.

That's when Don came in. "I'm surprised you're back so soon," he said. "But I know you wanted to, and we're glad to have you back." He'd lost a few people close to him, most significantly his daughter to breast cancer. We may have disagreed about how to handle my show, but I could now see on this we could agree.

After Kerry and Don walked away to their desks, Aaron was still looking at me. He cocked his head to the side, smiled, raised an eyebrow. "You okay?"

I smiled. "No. But that's okay."

We perfunctorily went over the guests for that day. I was a robot, reading out time codes, not present. *Today, on* Sense of Place*: listen in at Roundhouse Radio 98.3 as Minelle tries to pretend that everything is fine, when nothing is fine, nothing will be fine again! Coming up next: news with Kerry Marshall. Stay with us.*

I was lucky, though, because my team understood this and took the lead. My script was written out for me, word for word. The intro, the questions — everything. They knew I couldn't operate. They handed the notes to me, and I took them silently. The unspoken arrangement. We ended up doing this for months, frustration growing in them and complacency growing in me.

But on that first day back, the producer I worked with asked, with sincere concern, "Minelle, do you have it all?"

"Yes, yes, thank you," I said absent-mindedly. My body was there, at the mic, but my mind was somewhere else: still by my mother's hospital bed, watching her ragged breathing. I saw the yellow of her eyes, the mottling of her skin. "That's when you know she is about to go," the nurses told me quietly. "When the skin begins to mottle." The purple blotches, beginning at her heels, spreading up to her toes. *Don't think about it.*

I went through the questions but didn't hear the answers. But I knew this numbness must be short-lived; I knew I had to get back to work.

It was Kirk who helped me do so on that first day back. He was not a hugger, nor did I want him to be. I would have been afraid to ruffle his perfectly pressed shirt. But he gave me the greatest gift he could give me: a dream interview.

"Ruth Reichl is coming in to do a pre-tape with me at two p.m.," he said. Kirk normally liked to do the A-list interviews with the big stars, politicians, pundits and authors himself, and I didn't blame him for that one bit.

"Uh-uh, she's coming in to do a pre-tape with *me!*" I joked. Ruth was one of my heroes. She had saved me several times in my life.

Kirk saw that I was glassy-eyed, zombie-like. Maybe because I looked so rough, he caved. I couldn't believe it — the interview was mine! I did some quick calculations while fireworks went off in my head. *Sense of Place* finished at noon, which would leave me almost two hours to prep. *Yes, yes, I can do it.* I recognized a feeling inside me stirring, imbued with adrenalin. It was a dim feeling of excitement.

Ruth Reichl is a cookbook author and the author of several memoirs about her life as a food critic. Her publicist called and said that Ruth would be late and that she was hungry. I immediately thought of the new diner down the street. I'd gotten to know the staff there a little. I ran over, and when I arrived, out of breath, asked to speak to the chef. He came out wiping his hands on his apron. I said breathlessly, "Would you like to cook something small for Ruth Reichl?"

He looked at me, open-mouthed. I could see I'd already lost him: his mind had travelled to the land of a million recipes. He disappeared behind the counter and started throwing together a Thai soup, the scent of which lingered in the air: lemongrass, bird's-eye chili. I heard the sound of the spices sizzling in the wok. It was a sumptuous, fragrant dish, and I proudly took it back to the studio, whorls of steam enveloping me, cloaking me in a pungent perfume.

It was hard to stop the spectre of my mother's death from entering into my prep work. Reichl has spoken frankly about her fraught relationship with her mother and about her mother's death. I was convinced I could leave my own grief at the door, though, not bring it into the conversation — I could be professional. *You can do it, Mahtani.* Of course, that's when I heard my own words from my academic work come in, the words of critical journalists: objectivity is but a myth. And, as my friend Josh reminded me, objectivity is not only a myth, but one we construct through professional rituals. I had written about this in countless papers and have spoken about it a lot here already. But I still felt pressure to leave my story buried. The interview was about Reichl, not me. This was not the time to be blanketed in grief.

When Reichl arrived with her publicist, I nervously handed the author her soup. She was resplendent in bright colours, a shocking pink top, with a mass of ringlets and that unmistakable New York twang in her voice. She was hungry, she said, and this would hit the spot. She took a sip and pronounced it not only delicious but one of the best soups she'd had in a while. I did a happy dance in my head and made a mental note to share the good news with the chef.

When Reichl and I got behind the mics, I asked the questions I expected readers wanted me to ask: Why write this book now? What inspired it? All the drab questions that would be asked on any show she went on. But I also gave myself a little leeway. Her book revealed itself as a kind of in-between book, between stories, written when she was between jobs. I asked her about that kind of instability, that liminal space. I knew I was asking for myself, really. I was nervous, I was unstable, and I could feel it. I felt it in the overly long introduction I'd read out at the top of the segment — another living eulogy to bear witness to my raw grief — during which she'd waited, generously, for me to finish. Later, Chuck would force me to listen to it, the whole damned thing, and tell me just how sycophantic I sounded.

But when the interview finished, I felt flushed and happy. It wasn't my best work, but I had done it and I was proud of myself. Just before she left the studio, I asked Reichl to sign my copy of her book. She looked at me closely and gently asked me if I was all right.

Reichl has seen her share of grief, and I think she recognized that grief in me. She worked now from the scar, not the wound. Mine was still bleeding.

Shaken, thrown by her perspicacity, I stuttered, "My mom died two weeks ago."

Something dark crossed her face. She smiled, sighed. And then took the Sharpie from my hands and signed my book.

What she wrote isn't important. It was the look she gave me before she wrote it, and the look she gave me after, snapping the cover tight, that matters.

Memories and Grief

What they don't tell you about mourning is that it changes the way you remember. It changes how you speak about remembering too. Things shift from present tense to past tense. You have to count on colonial grammar to speak about the presence of your parent.

And your memories – they change too. They now come tinged with nostalgia. Maybe in your grief you remember just a little more fondly than you need to; maybe you exaggerate a fine detail to make someone look good, to make your memories of them make you look good too.

Your hardest memories – those are the ones you want to bury, and maybe, in some cases, you're able to. But death won't hide them from you forever. They are still there, lying in wait.

Polaroids

I was twenty-three. I was home during a short break from my studies in London, and I was staying with my mother. The tension between us had only increased as I'd moved farther and farther away. I still blamed her for leaving my dad, and I took every opportunity to be cruel to her in ways loud and quiet. Still, I came home to see her. Maybe out of guilt more than anything else. After an afternoon out to see friends in the city, I opened the front door of her place to discover her sitting at the living room table, Polaroid photos laid out in rows in front of her. About a hundred headshots, lined up ten by ten.

They were not just people. They were men. All Brown men, Muslim, some looking fairly dour, some smiling. Most in their best suits.

"I did *istikhara* for you. I contacted an auntie in our community. It is time to start looking. These are all men who are looking for a wife."

"You did *what?*"

"What's the harm, *beti*, in just looking, right? You're of that age . . . Why don't you just look at a few of these men? They come from good families, good backgrounds. Why not, *junam?*"

At this, I banged my fist on the table. It scared both of us, my sudden rage. "How could you do this?" I raised my voice a little louder. "You didn't have an arranged marriage! You married the furthest thing from it! Why would you want to do this to me?"

And with one look, she told me all I need to know: her own marriage had failed after she'd found love herself. What she wanted for me was greater certainty of stability, of happiness. To get what she never had. But I was too filled with arrogance to acknowledge this, and instead I grasped at the emotion more readily available to me: indignation, an emotion I had come to rely on more and more when I was with her. An emotion that veils fear.

"There is no way I am choosing anyone from this pile!" I swept my hands through the photos, and they cascaded to the ground. "I can choose my own partner!" I stamped to the front door and relished the sound the slam made, shaking the foundations of the house.

When I returned a few hours later for my encore performance, I saw that the photos had been scooped up from the ground. The living room table was now bare, no trace of what had happened left behind.

My mother never mentioned the photographs again, and neither did I.

But neither of us forgot. Even if I wish I could.

Forty Days

Dimly, in the recesses of my mind, I remembered that I was supposed to do something to commemorate her at the mosque forty days after her death. I wasn't sure what though. I hadn't asked her and she hadn't told me.

I emailed some of my scholarly Islamic studies friends to ask them. They said they had no idea, but one person kindly put me touch with another Islamic scholar in Vancouver. She also didn't know about the ceremony, but she still met me at a SkyTrain station so she could take me to the mosque. I struggled to remember a time I'd been to a mosque without my mom. I wasn't sure I ever had. I felt anxious about going on my own, without her.

The rain was pelting down, and the scholar unlocked the passenger door of her car for me. I handed her a gift: a scented candle I'd brought to say thank you. The scent permeated the car. We drove in the ceaseless rain to the mosque. When we arrived, she took me into the prayer area for women. The place was deserted. She gestured to me to pray. I hadn't even brought a prayer mat, but at least I had a scarf.

I bent down, started to pray. *Bismillah Hir Rahman Nir Rahim.* I wasn't sure what I was supposed to feel, but I wasn't feeling it. I rotated through the required prayers, and then I awkwardly stood, motioned to her that I was ready to go.

It didn't feel like enough. Was it enough? It felt like empty grasping, my hand reaching out to her when I knew she wasn't there. I remembered the words of Lydia Davis: "In the word *precarious* is prayer." I wasn't sure if I understood Davis correctly, but that idea, of being precarious while praying, spoke to me. Everything I did, said, now felt so precarious, tentative, fragile. Broken.

As we left the mosque, I thought about what I'd just done in my mother's name. Was this what she'd wanted me to do? How would I know if I had done it right?

Years later, thinking about this moment, I googled, "40 days after death ceremony, Islam," and this popped up on a message board: "Any Muslims that do commemorate the 40th day after death are doing something not sanctioned by Islam, and most probably following the custom of Hindu culture."

I laughed. *How telling*, I thought. That even through her death, she was dancing with my father, my Hindu dad — engaging both cultures. In death, as in life. She continued to mix cultures, through me.

The Orange Folder

It was March 2016, not even two months since her death. I should have been feeling better by then. Isn't that the way mourning works? I'd had my ceremony, the rituals . . . Surely it was time for the healing.

My team was patient with me, still writing out scripts for me to read verbatim on air. On this day, they'd scheduled an interview I wasn't sure I wanted to do. The sales team, normally careful to steer clear of editorial decisions, had changed their tune and asked us to interview a world-renowned psychic who had a big show happening at a sports arena that weekend. I was to welcome in calls from listeners who were yearning to hear from dead loved ones. I felt dubious about the call-in segment, but I did it anyway.

The psychic, it turned out, wasn't too woo-woo for me, and I didn't mind the segment at the start. The calls steadily streamed in. Calls from family members desperate to know how their grandfather was doing on the other side, or those who wanted to reach out to a beloved dead poodle. We got a call from someone whose son had died by suicide. *How is he doing now? Is he happy? Please tell me he's content. Please.*

Abruptly the psychic turned to me. "Minelle, I understand you've recently lost your mother."

No, I hadn't told her. My team said they hadn't either.

"She wanted me to tell you to go to the dentist because she thinks not going was one of the major culprits that led to her demise. Also, she wants you to go home and look for a bright orange folder. In it, there's something of yours she wants you to see."

Orange folder. Orange folder? I babbled something about how we were going to take a short break and would be right back. I was discombobulated, I admit. I was also skeptical. My mother wouldn't keep anything bright orange around, not even a blanket in the closet. Despite my attempts to be logical, though, I found myself drifting toward the space of the unknowing.

I pretty much forgot about the psychic's pronouncement for a few weeks, until I finally mustered up enough courage to go back to Toronto to finish the laborious process of cleaning up her affairs. I opened the front door of her house to the odour of mothballs combined with the stench of the litter box from my brother's two cats — it overwhelmed me and I gagged.

Everywhere, in all places and corners, were memories of her: the cracked turquoise Persian vases from her home in Abadan; the watercolours my grandfather painted; her lush, prized Persian rugs hanging from the walls on hooks, meticulous artwork. Bills with plastic windows lay like dishevelled playing cards on the hallway table, begging to be opened. I brushed them aside to deal with them later and slowly walked up the stairs to her bedroom.

My brother and I talked until the wee hours, and I tried on a bunch of my mom's clothing — the things I hadn't already packed up after the funeral — to see if I could keep anything. It made me feel closer to her. Her perfume was still on them. They were all beautiful — blazers and caftans, dresses and scarves. It was close to one a.m. at this point.

While I brazenly modelled in the mirror, my brother said he hadn't had any direct messages from our mom. I'd had a few dreams, so I airily said, "Oh, she'll make her presence known to you."

I wiped away a tear or two while I was packing away her Chanel-inspired bolero jackets — they were gold-buttoned, shiny, colourful.

I folded up her delicate scarves, saving a few, and unceremoniously stuffed the rest into a garbage bag to take to Goodwill. I was suddenly drawn to another bedroom, so I allowed myself to roam. My gaze was pulled to the bottom of a bookshelf. I blurrily thought to myself, to someone, *Show me what I need to see.*

My eye caught on a faded orange cloth folder with a batik pattern, next to my high school yearbook. I slid the folder out, slowly. It was frayed around the edges. I opened it up and found letters. Lots of them. They were stained and soft, dog-eared airmail letters. You know the old-fashioned ones, light blue with a red and white motif on the edges. There were letters from my grandmother to my mother, and letters from my uncle to my mother. They were written in fountain pen, scrawled on thin onion skin paper. They fell to the ground, so many of them.

A large envelope fluttered out too. On it, in my mother's handwriting, were the words "A Letter to My Children." I opened it carefully. Inside, there were eight copies of a poem she seemed to have printed from the internet. I know because I counted. It read:

Although you cannot see me,
Although my spirit's passed,
I walk with you from room to room
And will until the last.
Please know that I am safe here.
All pain is washed away.
I feel now only love for you
Every minute, every day.
When next we meet it will be
In this heaven like no other.
But always I will be to you
Your proud and loving mother.

I rushed out and showed it to my brother. I was grinning jubilantly. As he scanned it, he rolled his eyes. I know it's corny, but I can't help myself — I still think it was meant to be.

"Minelle, you see signs everywhere," he said. "This doesn't mean anything."

"Come on!" I said, while dancing a little two-step side shuffle. "It must mean something!"

My brother said, with a sigh, "You gotta get a grip."

The Limits of Linear Thinking

But why not read into everything?

I'd stupidly assumed that all the knowledge I needed to get over my grief was to be found in the piles of probate papers, the insurance letters, the bank accounts, the family albums, the diaries. But what about the other places I never thought to look?

My mother's death revealed the limits of my linear thinking. I had assumed that origin stories are easy to follow: first there is life and then there is death, a straight arrow, a line from A to Z clearly demarcated. Now I know that A to Z was never a straight line to begin with. The arithmetic of death was showing me another way to add and subtract, multiply and divide. Her death allowed for another presence to be made known in my life – the subtraction that makes way for addition.

Feathers

It was around this time that I became even more obsessed with feathers. Ever since I'd bought that necklace at the Vancouver airport, I'd kept thinking about them. I didn't dare remove the necklace. I wasn't sure why.

I kept seeing feathers everywhere. Presumably because it was almost springtime, and the birds were moulting. But that year, I kept *noticing* them. I caught glimpses of them on the street, near wet sewer grates or gently floating on the wind, caught in the breeze. They seemed to be all over the place, but most particularly when I asked the questions. The questions that quietly haunted me, the ones I dared not ask out loud.

Will I see you again?

The answer took the shape of a black crow's feather spattered with blue salt-ridden snow on a sidewalk near our home.

Are you doing all right?

The answer in the form of a delicate sparrow feather, curled up on the curb.

And the question I am embarrassed to admit that I asked:

Do you still love me?

The response: a bulky, healthy large seagull feather lying on our welcome mat.

The feathers had come to represent to me a kind of conversation with her — as if they were stories she wanted to share, signposts that she was fine, resting, happy, alive in her own way.

I strung the feathers together in my heart and mind. Sometimes I even brought them into the house where I stuck the dirty, ugly remnants into a pocked rock I'd found on the shoreline near Sooke. Sylvia came by, noticed the rock with the mottled and matted feathers poking out of it, dirtying my dresser, and exclaimed, "Minelle! That's revolting! How many germs must be on that thing . . . Please get rid of it!"

I tuned her out while muttering *yes, yes, sure I'll do it.* I knew I never would. Soon my dresser was overpopulated with these dank, dark feathers. But I kept them there. They are there still. Please don't judge me. Although I judge myself.

I spotted a coffee-table book at a bookstore. It was titled, simply, *Feathers.* The author, an artist, took feathers and carved gorgeous designs out of them. The artwork was stunning. I ended up having him on my show. He came into the studio all the way from Olympia, Washington. I timidly handed him a few of the feathers I had gathered that spring. I'm not sure what I was thinking. I guess that maybe he could carve something out of them. Not unkindly, he said, "I can't really carve things with those street feathers. But thank you." *Street feathers!* I loved this. The urban bird.

He handed me his book, and I opened it — out fluttered a bouquet of feathers, spotted, colourful and tiny. They decorated the radio desk; some fell to the ground.

In the interview, he told me that feathers are prophetic — that they tell a story.

Whenever I see a feather now, I am even more convinced she is present, she is with me.

I look forward to seeing her everywhere. Some days, no message; other days, many.

The question on my lips:

Is every feather just a prayer being carried home?

The Sound of Feathers

Years later I would find myself in White Rock, British Columbia, where the crests of frosted white waves crashed loudly against the shoreline during a bitterly cold November. Sitting on a patio by the water, I noticed an errant red geranium blossom fluttering by, mobilized by a sudden ocean breeze. What was that delicate thing doing there? It wasn't the season for it. I was brought back to the bright red potted geranium on the stairs of my old apartment on Amity Street in Brooklyn, my mind in two geographies at once. Ruby blossom. Little red cardinal. My friend Candis's words: "The water, the world, the birds, the stones, the rocks, the rain, the water, the plants, the flowers." Every story, always another story.

I idly flipped through a book of Persian poetry edited by Niloufar Talebi. A poem by the poet, essayist and translator Yadollah Roya'i caught my eye:

Sun-baked clay, and a skull in the midst of
feathers, with an archfeather in each eye hole,
and there is nothing anywhere, not even
mother's name, in the feather's sound.

My velvet robin's breast puffed out with pride. My mind returned to that rock on my dresser, the rock dotted with feathers, so etched by sand and sea and wind, the rumblings of the tide. I felt exonerated by those words, redeemed. *Finally, finally, finally.*

Across the patio, a mother sipped on a takeout coffee, her baby twins in matching car seats beside her. She caught me wiping away my salty tears and looked at me with concern: *Are you okay?* I nodded, and by mutely responding I was speaking back to her, and to countless generations of mothers before us, and after us, delicately tracing their histories and futures with my wordless words, saying what needed to be said without saying anything at all.

Breastfeeding II

Flipping through a magazine one day, I saw an illustration of a woman's bare breasts. The muscles were exposed, exempt of skin. It was an image of the winding milk duct circuitry around the breast. It really was a wonder! It looked like little flowers, or tiny hearts. Its architecture was spellbinding, beautiful. I revelled in its glory, its curlicues. I thought a lot about that image. It wasn't until later that I found out the picture was fraudulent. Turns out the milk duct system isn't actually shaped like the intricate branches of trees, the stems of leaves, of clover. Turns out the truth is much more prosaic.

"Those flower-shaped things are definitely not ducts," I read on ScienceAlert.com. "They probably represent the lobules, except in a real human breast they are not arranged in such a neat pattern at all."

Because, of course, a woman's body can't look like that, right? We are not neat, tidy.

After she died, years after I'd stopped breastfeeding, a few droplets of milk suddenly made an appearance. They fell unceremoniously from my breast in the shower, making a tiny opaque misshapen puddle on the floor.

Do You Really Want to Know?

This is the part I'm embarrassed to tell you.

A few months after she was gone, I was surprised at how I was feeling. No longer comatose, I cycled between two very different emotional spaces. These spaces weren't sadness or even depression, or what I thought grief should feel like. I experienced euphoria one minute, and nothing the next. No in-between. I was getting up at six a.m. with a renewed sense of energy. I normally hit my snooze button four or five times each morning. But now? I was bounding out of bed, running every day, pounding the pavement across from the seawall on Kitsilano Beach, watching the sun rise. I was preparing lunches for my family before they even got up. I had all the patience in the world for my son. I was cranking out scripts in minutes. I laughed easily, loudly. This, I had not anticipated.

After watching my mother suffer for months, I had a different understanding of the guises of grief. I was, truthfully, happy not to be stuck in the hospital any longer, so glad not to be waiting for the death that seemed it would never arrive. Until it did. What a surprising and shocking recognition: that it would bring me deep-sighing comfort to know it was over.

The much-awaited consolation prize of death.

The Year of Firsts

Along with my new-found energy came a marked determination to produce a stronger and sleeker show. I was convinced the show could be great! Really amazing! If only I put more of myself into it. If only we put more of *ourselves* into it, I told my team, meaningfully.

They looked back at me with blank stares. *What are you talking about? How much more can we do?*

I chastised myself for not paying closer attention to Chuck's advice, admonished myself for not practising my vocal exercises like Kerry had told me to. I started to do them at work while I sat across from him. "*A, E, I, O, U.*" I recited them again before I went on air.

"Minelle, you don't need to do that any more," Kerry said and winked. "You're fine."

But I ignored him and tried to find ways to be better. I had to be.

I started to read even more voraciously, looking for stories I could cover. Angles that had been missed by other outlets. I forced my staff to look for new stories too. What I conveniently forgot was that they were all exhausted. They'd been grinding it out daily while I was sitting by my mother's bedside watching her die. Plus, our funding had been cut by the board. The station was not doing as well as everyone had hoped. And now I was asking them to do more? It was an outrageous request, to be sure, but it took me years to figure that out. I became the eye-rolling martyr who grew visibly annoyed when they couldn't book the guests I wanted. ("So what about the time difference! We can just stay later!") When their answers were less satisfactory to me, I harrumphed and said, "I'll do it myself then."

I started to book guests without their help, and the system became unworkable when folks got double-booked. We had to undo interviews that had been scheduled. I began to see my team looking at me scornfully. On the worst day, after I had dumped some of my best passive-aggressive behaviour on them, I caught them whispering about going to some opening-night gala together. I thought about confronting them: why they hadn't invited me? But why would they? I'd been an asshole the last few months. I wouldn't have invited me either.

Just when I was feeling ready to break, the front-desk receptionist came over with a bouquet of flowers. They were lilies of the valley — my very favourite. *This must be from someone who really knows me*, I thought.

They were from my cousin in New York. The note said, "Happy birthday to Ameh today. Thinking of you as I know you must miss her! With so much love to you. Family, family, family."

That was right. I'd forgotten. It was July 12. My mother's birthday.

The year of firsts: her first birthday, my birthday, the first Eid and Nowruz without her.

I didn't tell anyone why I'd received flowers. I just kept my head down, prepping for the show the next day, always another show.

Oak Leaf

Shortly after she died, I took myself out for a walk one night. The moon was out. It was late February, and there was a smattering of dirty snow on the ground. The sidewalks were treacherous, and I stumbled on something.

I looked down. It was a piece of frozen dog excrement. I started to curse inwardly and then became incensed. *Why can't people pick up after themselves? What is wrong with people? The world is just too cruel. What's the point of living? It's outrageous that people won't take care of themselves, each other!* I ranted and raged. And I tried to take the remnants off my boot, shaking it angrily.

Then I looked a little closer. It was not what I thought. It was a baby maple leaf. Actually, I was wrong again. It was a glossy brown oak leaf. In the moonlight, the crystals on the leaf shimmered brightly.

It was beautiful.

I just missed it.

I missed it all.

Prayer Book

Now that my mother is gone, it's her voice I long to hear. The photos I have of her aren't enough. To be sure, I appreciate the images: her posing in her gorgeous chiffon saris with perfectly applied lipstick. For anyone lucky enough to catch a glimpse of her, her beauty is clear.

I miss all the sounds of her voice, its high and low ranges. And what makes my heart break is knowing I will never hear that voice again, never hear the stories of her childhood: how she got into medical school but never finished, why she married my father and, Lord, the biggest question — why she adored me so much. And it wasn't just because I was her daughter. That's the easy answer.

What I found much later, scrawled in her precious dog-eared Islamic prayer book, the book she had inscribed to me, knowing it would come to me after she died: "My darling Muni, my life, my love, my best friend. Thank you for saving me. xoxoxo"

I will always regret the questions I never asked her, questions I didn't ask not only because I was afraid of the answers, but because of my own naive certainty that I would have time to ask her those questions later, as if later was a destination I could always eventually travel to. Now later is gone, I will never go there, I never got a ticket, and those words she never said, that voice I will never hear again — history.

The Problem with Listening

I finally went to see a therapist. I told myself it was only because of the freight of the interviews with activists and authors, that heavy burden, or because I had become cross at home, impatient with my little boy, picking fights with Bruce, with my colleagues. But, of course, it was more than that.

I got an email from a friend. She wrote, "My nerves would be shot if I were in your chair."

I was lucky. I got an appointment with a renowned Indigenous therapist. Shirley sat across from me, in a comfy chair, and handed me Kleenex as I wiped away tears. I explained what I do on the show. I told her I was exhausted. The listening was overwhelming me. I couldn't hear these stories. I couldn't hear them anymore.

She listened and then said, "The problem isn't how you are listening. It's your personal geography. You need to shift how you sit in the studio."

I wasn't sure what she meant.

"Right now you're sitting across from your guests, and you are ingesting their stories. They are becoming part of you. Their stories are taking up space in you, as they share that story with you. You need to have your guest sit farther away from you, and after, you pick up the stories they shared," she gestured, "and sweep them to the ground. Take the stories and return them to the earth. The next day, do the same thing, over and over again."

It was about my relation to story. Her method was a cultural way of responding to story, of recognizing the power of stories and of seeing the land as an ally and repository for story.

I tried to imagine ways to summon my mother with me into that room, like a small delicate brown sparrow perched precariously on my shoulder.

Counting

There was another thing that was bothering me that I didn't want to admit to you.

The counting — I told you about it before, right? How I was always counting?

It had gotten worse.

I'd played this game since I was a kid. I felt it was guaranteed to predict the future. It was almost never wrong. I added numbers over and over again. Phone numbers, street addresses . . . If they added up to seven or fourteen, something wonderful would happen — or more accurately, nothing bad would. Fifteen was okay too. Thirteen portended doom. My own name — Minelle Mahtani — seven and seven letters, respectively. I read somewhere that the number seven symbolizes spiritual perfection. Farideh — seven too. So, Mom was in the clear. At least with her name. Maybe not with her fate.

The number of our house before my parents divorced: 240. Adds up to six. A safe number, not seven, but close.

The number of her hospital room: 333. Too many threes.

The bill from the clinic in Germany: $23,215. A fifteen in there, but if you add up all the numbers, it's thirteen and that is just bad news.

The counting took on a new ominous form once she was gone. I started to scour licence plates for clues. If the numbers on the plate added up to thirteen, I was in trouble. The day would be over, terrible, disastrous. But if they added up to fourteen: bliss. And what this ultimately meant was simple: thirteen meant she was unhappy in Heaven; fourteen or fifteen meant she was okay, fine, hanging out with her mother and my dad, maybe drinking a gin and tonic now that it wasn't haram or maybe planting geraniums in her garden. If I saw a plate that looked at a glance like it might add up to thirteen, I averted my gaze.

It became impossible to go for a walk — it took me forever to count the different numbers I encountered, my fingers absentmindedly tapping on my lap as I strolled.

Mama, why are your fingers dancing on your legs?

No reason, junam. *No reason.*

PFT 035 — that added up to eight. Safe. Neutral. Not good, not bad. Just there. But actually, that wasn't all. *P* is sixteen. *F* is six. And *T* is twenty. Twenty plus sixteen plus six is forty-two. Four plus two is six. Still pretty neutral. So all that was . . . okay. Fine. Nothing bad would happen that day.

QS1 2J3 — jackpot. Twelve plus three is fifteen. Fifteen is the new fourteen. That meant not only would everything be okay, but everything would be *more* than okay. Remember that sixteen is only neutral. Same as twelve, but twelve is not as good as sixteen. Seventeen has a special place in my heart because it is ten plus seven, seven being my favourite because Minelle has seven letters and so does Mahtani and so does Farideh. Nineteen makes me irrationally annoyed, but still it isn't thirteen, which, if you have been paying attention, is to be avoided at all costs.

JU5 62T — uh-oh, trouble on the horizon. Watch where you step. There might be a hole in the ground waiting to swallow you whole. Maybe you will get an email with some bad news, like the cancer diagnosis of someone you love. It's not good news, that's for sure.

You see how these numbers tell me a story about my world in a way that no therapist or doctor or friend or astrologist can. The numbers illuminate the future, predict it. The numbers won't lie to me. They are out there making an offering. I have to listen to them.

Eavesdropping

The station was not doing well financially. The plan for its commercial success had fallen apart; the old-school approach of hiring salespeople to sell ad airtime was just not flying. Kirk sometimes grumbled about this, wondered why we didn't have a better social media campaign. I had lobbied for bus advertisements featuring Kirk and me: *Tune in to the morning shows, with Kirk at 6 and Minelle at 10!* But bus ads, like other kinds of ads, turned out to be too expensive. The station was hemorrhaging money.

I should have read how dire things were from the way Don's face was etched with worry. But I didn't. I kept my head down and tried to work.

One day, I eavesdropped on Don speaking on the phone. I heard the words "application . . . master's . . . Simon Fraser . . . hard to get into . . . worth a try . . ."

It dawned on me. *Is Don trying to go back to school? Could he have been talking about himself?*

Ever the journalistic sleuth, I started googling and up came the master's program at SFU. Turned out one didn't need to have a BA to get in.

Don's behaviour toward me had shifted since I'd come back to work after my mom's death. I thought he was feeling sympathetic, knowing first-hand how excruciating grief can be from grieving his daughter. But maybe it was something else too.

Don had been hosting his own show the last little while. Called *Impact*, the program showcased prominent NGO leaders who were making a difference. I had vaguely wondered what had fuelled his passion to create this program; I rarely listened to it, too busy focusing on my own show. But maybe, just maybe, his interviews were having an impact on him. I didn't give it much thought until later.

Later being the day Trump won the election.

Lewis Gordon and Fanon

The day before the world upended, I went home from work relaxed and well prepped. Everyone anticipated a Clinton win, so I'd booked some straightforward interviews for the next day: a few feminist scholars would come on to speak about what it meant to have a woman president in the United States. To be followed by a piece about a new knitting course — something like that. We also had a movie review scheduled.

A colleague had invited Bruce and me to watch the poll numbers come in with him and his partner. We sat in front of their TV in shock as we watched the numbers creep higher and higher for Trump, the screen filling with more and more red, less blue. I watched for a while, horrified, then said, "I have to get home. I can't run tomorrow's show the way I planned. I have to change everything."

Bruce and I went home, and I hit the phone.

My first call: "Don, this is not going to turn around. I have to reprogram my show."

Don: "You'll have to do this yourself, you know. There's no time to get everyone going on this."

And he was right. There just wasn't enough time.

I thought for a moment. *What am I going to do? How can I talk about a new knitting course when Trump is about to be elected president of the United States? What would Mom say?* I kept thinking about Trump's point of view on immigrants and how his perspective would have devastated her. I went into autopilot and started calling critical race theorists I knew and begging them to come on the show to speak about what a Trump win would mean for Americans. I watched the election results roll in with my phone in one hand, my remote control in the other, switching from one news channel to another, praying I was just reading the screen wrong. Bruce kept walking out of the room, coming back in, shaking his head at the screen. He was too shocked for words. His worst nightmare had come to life. I spent the evening distracting myself, avoiding the pain of a potential Trump win by reproducing my entire show.

The mood in the station the next day was ghastly. No one said a word to me. But I walked into the studio knowing exactly what I wanted to say in my intro. I sat behind the mic, cleared my throat and this is what came out.

"Good morning, everyone. It's a sombre morning here at *Sense of Place*. A lot of tears, and tempers have flared. I think most of us are still numb, trying to make sense of the seemingly nonsensical. But let's be clear: it's not as nonsensical as we might think. Donald Trump's victory yesterday was a successful attempt among angry and exasperated white voters to halt the social progress that was ushered in by Barack Obama's presidency. This is a major score for white supremacy. Fact. Cold retaliation toward a country that voted for a Black president and had the audacity to try to leave the racial politics of the last two centuries behind.

"Today's show will look at hope in a time of seeming hopelessness. We try to sift through the chaff and ask, How did this happen? And what can we do about it? We don't have the luxury to mourn. Our guests today, ranging from a journalist on the ground in Florida to an African American scholar in Texas, will share with us how we grapple and keep on keepin' on in the face of what seems to be an utterly hopeless day."

I looked up from my notes and saw Don staring at me solemnly through the studio glass. Was he mad at me? Was he going to come in and tell me to stop? But then I watched as he slapped my copy of philosopher Lewis Gordon's book *What Fanon Said* in the window. I teared up. In response, Don returned my gaze: sternly, seriously. It was a call to arms, a sign of resistance, a salvo.

Looking back now, I can see that this was the moment that things changed between us. It's true — we were an odd combination: him all bravado and swagger, and me always ready with a wagging finger and cocked hip to call out racism at a moment's notice. But with this small, quiet gesture, Don said everything I needed to hear to get me through that day's show. And I did.

Epigenetics

Jean stood by my fridge as I poured her a meadow-tinged glass of Sauvignon Blanc. We were still friends these many years later. One of the nice things about being in Vancouver was that we now lived in the same city. I told her I kept wondering what had happened to my mom's body after she died. I almost told her about the counting — but I didn't dare.

As we lose our loved ones, those beloved bodies, how do we cope? The ritual of counting to soothe the trauma. Trauma as question, ritual as answer. I believed that the ritual of counting was the answer that would save me from the trauma. Maybe it was okay for me to count; maybe I didn't have to pathologize myself any more than I already did. Why was the counting different from the feathers, from the other ways I sought solace? My anxieties and the things I did to try to keep myself safe . . . the things that didn't keep me safe anymore.

Jean and I moved on to the subject of the body and its link to grief and trauma. She said, "We're really only just discovering that trauma can skip a generation or two. That some genes become active or dormant, and it's not only a person's environment but also their individual decisions that can alter the expression of their genes and thus influence the lives of their descendants."

This reminded me of the words of my friend Alicia, who says in her book *A Mind Spread Out on the Ground*:

> This world does not belong to you; you are merely borrowing it from the coming faces. Epigenetics seems to replicate that philosophy on the genetic level. Your decisions and traumas are never solely yours alone, or even yours and your children's. Your decisions and traumas mark every subsequent generation after you, creating ripples in the future that can't always be anticipated and can never be controlled.

Which of my mother's stories were living in my body? Which had I passed on to my son?

Searching for Repair

Later, I landed an interview with Salman Rushdie. He didn't come into the studio, despite our bulletproof glass. I called him at his hotel; he went by a pseudonym, of course. The question I asked that has stayed with me is this one: "I want to make sure that we talk about the issue of repair before we end today. One of my favourite lines in your book is again uttered by Riya who says, 'My field [. . .] should be a soft safe place for understanding. Instead it's a war zone. I choose peace.' I want to ask you how do we do that daily, that process of repair. What does that look like for you — that process of repair?"

Rushdie took a beat. I could hear him clear his throat. He answered slowly. "I'm trying to think how best to answer that. One of the things I think about the characters in this book is that we are all damaged. You know, life damages the living, and the people in this book carry within themselves various forms of damage, and try to live the best lives they can in carrying those wounds. And if they are lucky, they're able to heal. If they're extra lucky, they find somebody who can help them heal. Or they find a place that is nourishing . . . but I do think it's the story of human life that we are, you know, we are all beaten up by life. We all carry those bruises. Some of us to a greater degree than others, and certainly one of the great subjects of literature is how human beings deal with that."

Beaten up, down, by life. Carrying bruises. The heavy cargo of stories. The subtle act of repair. I circled around his words for days after, his veiled way of speaking from experience. I crafted my own words, too, about choosing *repair* deliberately over other *R* words, like *reconciliation* and *reparation*, as if those practices could ever exist.

I wondered during that grieving time what repair would look like for me. Could I dare dream it would mean more than carrying the freight of intergenerational trauma? I prayed that it would.

Erica Violet Lee writes, "If historical trauma is strong enough to alter our DNA and remain in our bones for generations, then there is no question in my mind that the love of our ancestors is in our DNA and our bones as well. The memory of that love is strong enough that it still exists in us, and in the plants that we have always cared for." As Alicia Elliott asks, "And if intergenerational trauma can alter DNA, why can't intergenerational love?"

Rushdie helped me see that repair meant gathering close to my heart the other side of that pairing. It meant not just clutching the trauma but also allowing in the intergenerational gemstones — those kaleidoscopic, fracturing moments of light; inherited strengths that are more than wounds, but wealth.

Meal with a Stranger

Why does the death of my mother feel so different from the death of my father? It's not that one hit me harder than the other. But they did feel entirely different.

When my father died in 2006, ten years before my mother, I wandered the streets of Toronto aimlessly — long walks from my faculty apartment near the university to the north end of the city and back. I walked from Bloor and Spadina all the way to Eglinton to stave off the grief. But it wasn't going anywhere, not for a long while, chasing me down those city streets, making its presence known through a billboard he would have loved, an ad that would have made him laugh, a glimpse of someone who looked a little like him, but honestly not really if you looked hard enough.

Not much more than a month after he died, probably in May, when all those flowers burst into bloom despite the fact that he was gone, those gorgeous motherfucking flowers that had not had the good grace to know better, I walked into a bar near Yonge and Summerhill. The Rebel House. It was a snug watering hole with a back patio, offering local microbrews on tap and pub fare. I obeyed the grumbling in my stomach despite having no appetite; I had lost about ten pounds since his death. I knew I had to eat.

I sat down in one of the wooden booths and ordered a cheeseburger and a pint of cider. The place was almost empty on that weekday; there was one other person in the restaurant — an elderly man sitting across from me at the end of the bar. From the back, with his thatch of white hair peppered with just a little black, forest-green sweater, dark skin on the back of his neck, I thought he vaguely resembled my dad.

I had been seeing my father everywhere since he'd died but only for split seconds. Almost every elderly Indian man on the street reminded me painfully of him. I kept thinking of the word *vanish*. Because everything kept vanishing. My keys. My glasses. I kept seeing my dad and then in the next second — gone.

This man, this man who I couldn't really see, reminded me so much of my father.

My food came, and I ate without tasting a bite of it. Cardboard. When the bill came, I impulsively said to the waiter, "See that guy over there? Can you put his meal on my tab, as well?"

The waiter looked at the guy, then looked at me and grinned. "Little old for you, don't you think?" He raised his eyebrows, laughing at me but only a little.

"Nah, it's not that." I didn't know how to explain to him what I was doing. "Can you do it for me without telling him that it's from me? I'll leave first, 'kay?"

The waiter nodded, clearly used to crazy customers.

It wasn't a lot of money, maybe twenty-five dollars — the man had had a roast beef sandwich (something my dad would have eaten) and a pint of lager. I paid the bill and left.

Why am I telling you this story? Don't make the mistake of thinking I want you to feel sorry for me. In my hazy, grief-stained mind, it was simple: I was buying lunch for my dad. I was having lunch with my dad, together but separate.

Don in School

Since he'd pressed the book against the studio window, I'd noticed that Don had changed. He was calling me over frequently — not to berate me, as he so often had — but to read out a snippet of something from his MA program material: Martha Nussbaum, Michel Foucault, Michel de Certeau, Bruno Latour . . . Not Audre Lorde, not bell hooks — not yet. But they would come. He was falling in love with theory. And I was entranced watching him fall in love with the ideas that I'd fallen in love with years ago in grad school myself.

He started to say things like, "Minelle, remember you told me there won't be climate justice without racial justice and I told you that you were wrong? Well, now I see it's a five-alarm fire! We can't have one without the other!" He held up a dog-eared book by Naomi Klein, waving it in my face.

It felt like such a sudden shift to me, but of course it wasn't. He was looking at me with different eyes — with a little more, dare I say it, respect. I was a little annoyed that it'd taken Foucault and Nussbaum to bring him to this place, but that was just my own ego getting in the way again. I was happy he was feeling this way. Grateful, too, because his new perspective meant I had a lot more freedom in designing the show.

With this freedom, though, I was making even more demands of my team, and they were growing irate with my new-found grit and determination to take more control. I was demanding too much from them — not only in relation to the radical nature of our content but also in the specificity of my requests. *Find me a critical race scholar in Australia who can speak about the globalizing impact of Trump's win in their country. Why couldn't you book that director from* This Is Us *on the show?*

"Minelle, we can't book that guest," my producers would say.

But I wasn't listening. I was tapping out numbers on my notebook. "Yes, you can," I would say, not looking up. I was thinking, *Thirteen fifteen seventeen nineteen thirteen.*

I was wielding my voice like a scalpel. My producers looked tired. And the station was floundering. The murmurings in the office hinted that we only had a few more months on air before we went under. Like the loss of my mother, I was in denial about this too. Everyone was under strain: it felt like the world would crack under it all.

Jāt Khāli-yé

I was purchasing Cheerios for Cole at Whole Foods when I spotted a mother and her daughter buying treats together, heads bent, carefully contemplating what chocolate delicacy they wanted for a little picnic together. I started to cry, thinking of all those lost lunches, trips, shopping expeditions my mother and I never went on. I thought about how I always used to say to her, "We're going to Italy next year. I have points." And how we never went.

The Persian expression "*Jāt khāli-yé*" means, loosely, "You were missed."

My mother used to say it meant that a place at our table was empty. I googled it and found this on *Chai and Conversation*:

> Anytime you speak of an event or experience that was very enjoyable, but the person you are talking to was not present, you are obligated to tell them that they were missed in the situation. This way, they know you were thinking of them, and that it would have been better if they'd been there.
> Another way of saying this is *jāt sabzé*, which literally means "your place is green," or there is green grass growing where you should have been.

I remember when my friend Sheryl lost her mother. To try to nurse her cracked heart, she embarked upon a week-long cruise through the Norwegian fjords. Dark blue skies, frosty waves and ivory tundra accompanied her. I only know this because she sent me pictures of the bow cam at one-thirty a.m. "White nights," she texted, flourishing her message with a few well-earned exclamation marks.

She told me something else too. She said she had been eating dinner by herself every night at a table set for two.

"In fact, I've asked the wait staff not to remove the place setting," she texted. "I have wanted my table set for two, even though I am one."

And we both knew why.

Feeding Grief

Do you remember the last meal you ate with someone you loved before they died?

I remember the meals I ate with her. I remember making food after the memorial. But I don't remember our last meal together. I really wish I did.

My mom loved food so much that she was rendered mute by it on more than one occasion. You would know she loved something she was eating because she wouldn't say a word. She would just open her eyes wide, so wide.

I wish I had made sure she enjoyed more of the foods she loved before she lost the ability to savour them. To this day, I regret not bringing her a malted chocolate milkshake, a spoonful of hot sauce from her favourite Hakka restaurant. But most of all, I'm sure she hankered for the food from her childhood, which ended up becoming the food of my childhood too. *Hinjo*, that Burmese fish soup made with vermicelli. Remember I told you about it? My mouth waters, writing that down for you.

When Bruce, Cole and I moved neighbourhoods about six years after she died, I spotted a small restaurant on Victoria Drive near our new place. It was called Amay's House – Burmese cuisine. The day I noticed it I was walking back from a doctor's appointment, and icy rain was blanketing down, a typical Vancouver winter morning, and I was feeling sorry for myself. I was drenched, my worn MEC jacket doing nothing to keep out the chill. But spotting the restaurant, I immediately thought about my mother. As if propelled by another force, I went inside. A shih tzu resembling Simone was curled up on a dilapidated doggy bed in the corner; the staff was watching TV behind the counter. Every story, always another story.

When I saw the word *hinjo* burning brightly on the lit-up menu board above the counter, I didn't think twice. I ordered two containers of it and blurted out to the woman placing it into a white plastic bag for me, "This is my mom's favourite food!"

She smiled at me and said, "Then you must bring her in! And have her taste some of our other delicacies!" She started rattling off the names of other Burmese dishes I knew my mother also loved. But I was not listening — I was too struck by the fact that I'd used present tense to speak about her. I continued this charade for months.

Every time I dropped by, the lady behind the counter would ask, "When are you going to bring your mother in?" She would cluck, reprimanding me. "I will make her a special treat! Just for her!"

"Soon, soon . . ." I would say, not able to bring myself to tell her the truth.

Unfulfilled Promises

I told you I said I would take her to Italy, right?

I said a lot of things, turns out.

I said I would throw her a surprise party at eighty. She'd always wanted one, hinted at it for years.

I said I would say my prayers every day.

I said I would call my relatives more regularly — her brother, my aunts, my brother.

I said I would wear that saffron and fuchsia sari if I ever got married, the one she'd bought me in India when I was sixteen, the one with silver-sequined elephants embroidered on the cuffs.

I promised I would give my first cousin, her beloved niece, the plate with the cherubic face on it after my mother died. I can't find it anywhere in the storage locker. But maybe I haven't looked that hard.

I promised I wouldn't eat bacon again. This one I didn't promise her, really. I only promised it to myself after she died, and I haven't eaten it since. It was my favourite thing. My friend Karen nicknamed me Bacon on one camping trip years ago after seeing me scarf down slice after slice. And now I will never eat it again. I guess this last one is a promise fulfilled, for her.

The Hot Dog

On a trip to Toronto after her death, I discovered I had a rare night alone to myself in my haunted hometown. These were cherished and snatched moments — opportunities for me to revisit my geography of grief as I traversed my old streets. *Yes, there's the street lamp I leaned against at the corner of Sussex and Spadina when I talked to my dad for the very last time.* I don't know why I tortured myself by touring through tragedies in this way.

I turned north, away from the Annex toward Rosedale, along Davenport toward Le Paradis, eventually landing at the cozy French bistro. I must have been the youngest person in the restaurant. It was not a young person's haunt, but then again I wasn't young anymore. I was seated in the dining room. The dim light of the place made it feel peaceful. I noticed a print of the familiar Robert Doisneau photograph *Kiss by the Hôtel de Ville* hanging above me. Maybe you know it. It's pretty popular. It hung in my room for years as a teenager; the same print hung in my father's place after I moved out. Now it adorns the hallway of my brother's basement apartment.

Always more than one story.

I spent what felt like hours perusing the simple menu; it was that comforting to me. I swore to myself that I would eat something luxurious but healthy. But it was a French bistro, and everything was slathered in butter and salt. Oh, what a shame! I would just have to indulge. I opted for the most indulgent-sounding thing on the menu: steak bavette and frites. Extra mayo, please. Of course.

I ordered it rare, and it arrived ruby red, glistening on the plate. It looked inviting. I speared a forkful, prepared to savour every bite, but instead I found myself choking it down. Not even the gorgeous Pinot Noir by my side helped.

What is wrong with me?

Cancer, I realized. Luscious, velvety meat was gliding down my gullet, but my mom had been so sick at the end that she struggled to choke down fluids, even with a straw.

When she had just been diagnosed, I'd taken her to the Aga Khan Museum in Toronto, a place she had longed to visit. I chastise myself now for not taking her earlier. She pointed to pictures she loved, her long fingers showing me what she admired. Afterwards, we went to Costco so I could buy her a Vitamix blender to make smoothies. I bought eight pairs of black socks — socks I still own, now rife with holes but I refuse to throw them out. At the checkout, my mom wouldn't let me pay. We struggled over the bill like we always did. She dodged and weaved to hand her credit card to the cashier. She won that round, and it made her happy. She smiled a smile of victory.

As we rolled out with the cart, she stopped in front of the food vendor. "I think I need a hot dog," she said mischievously.

I stopped in my tracks. I didn't know whether to laugh or cry. I had told her for years that hot dogs cause cancer. It had been a running joke between us. "They're full of shit," I would say.

But she adored them. She loved coming into the city and stopping at one of downtown Toronto's many hot dog carts, dousing a toasted poppy seed bun with toppings: sauerkraut, ketchup, hot peppers. So many hot peppers. Her eyes, wide as dinner plates as she bit in. "But, Muni," she would say, laughing, mouth full. "These are halal! You should be happy!"

And every time, I would scold her. "No. No, Mom! Don't do it!" I would roll my eyes, shake my head, but also smile in recognition of her childlike wonder at the world.

And now I saw her, so thin, feebly making a joke about a damned hot dog, when I knew she could barely chew any longer.

She smiled.

Cut to that fancy French bistro, with its fancy white tablecloth, with its fancy fucking steak — and I just couldn't eat it. I just couldn't.

From: Minelle Mahtani

Hi everyone,

I'm looking at the rundown for tomorrow, and I have to admit I'm disappointed.

It shows that our production team is scrambling. What happened? I shouldn't have to come in to find that there are such significant holes on my show and that we're scrounging around at the last minute for guests. It feels rushed and uneven. I know we can do better. We're going to have to, if we want to stay on the air. I can't imagine Kirk's show goes without bookings like this — and that there are this many holes in his show.

For future reference, I want to make two points. First, if you're chasing up something, and your initials are beside a story, it's your responsibility to follow it up and make sure it is booked. Two, I will tell you if I want to put any of you on the air. We should only go there if we're really in a jam. There are more than two million people in this town. Surely everyone in our city has a story to tell. I'm feeling like we're all forgetting what

Sense of Place was meant to do and be. If so, here are eleven stories I'd like for us to follow up on. They all involve characters who have come up with an idea and have made that dream into a reality. They are one-offs. They can all be booked immediately. I appreciate your attention and time toward making *Sense of Place* sing again.

Sincerely,
Minelle

From: Sense of Place Team

TO: Minelle Mahtani

SUBJECT: RE: Holes on the show and show ideas for the future

Thanks Minelle – great ideas. Very helpful that you included
contacts as well.

That's it. That's all I got back.

I wondered who tapped into the group email and wrote it. I never
found out. I stewed for the rest of the show, walked out the door without saying a word.

Addition

The compulsive adding – it got worse. Its consumptive energy glittered darkly behind my eyes, its sharp edges chasing me on the peripheries of my perception.

On my way to work, I wouldn't get off the 4 bus until I saw a licence plate adding up to fourteen. If I caught even a glimpse of one that added up to thirteen, I couldn't get off at my regular stop. Not until I saw the right kind of plate. If I was lucky, I could get off at the Starbucks a stop away. When I didn't see what I needed, I ended up staying on past the viaduct and then I trudged back, an extra twenty-minute journey to the station. Some days I barely made it in on time, sweat on my brow, with only two minutes to spare before we were live. I even started to wear sneakers to work, stacking my heels in my purse to change into once I got to the studio, knowing I might have to make that crazed run in.

Whenever I was nearly late, Don glowered. But I didn't care. I was already wondering how I could make sure my gaze fell on the right plates the next day, to help determine my fate.

Arithmomania

"Arithmomania (from the Greek *arithmós*, 'number,' and *maniá*, 'compulsion') is a mental disorder that may be seen as an expression of obsessive-compulsive disorder (OCD). Individuals experiencing this disorder have a strong need to count their actions or objects in their surroundings," I read on Wikipedia.

The number of times I had to chew on one side of my mouth: five.

The number on the volume of the television set: seven.

The last four digits of my cellphone number at the time: 7184, which equals twenty.

People with this condition suffer from a rare form of OCD, a means of trying to gain control over powerless situations, I read.

In the repetition of it all, the safety of return.

But surely this was a situation where I could wrest control? I believed in this with an almost-religious sanctity: if I just kept counting, I could scientifically seduce the world into doing what I needed it to do. I believed it with a pulsating energy that clouded my mind and judgment.

Apocalyptic Numbers

13   19   3

3

17

14

3

3   3

3   13

13

7   3   13 7
5 1 2
6
13   13   14
11
2   19
13   3   17

15

17

13

2

15

7

4

17   12

3

2

11

3   7

14   15   13

15

6

2

3

33   14 17

7 3   3

13   13

3   19 3

15   15

7   7

this is how i know i am in trouble — when i only see the thirteens, the threes.

4

the sevens and the fourteens and fifteens only appear hazily at the corners of my consciousness and i pay them no mind. they are the lucky numbers, but i can't give them serious attention. they are decoys.

17

it is only the thirteens and threes in my line of sight.

the refusal to jump off the bus. the stopping on the stairs to rub my foot on the last step fourteen times. no matter how much i count, the numbers add up to the same conclusion.

11

14

No Number Fifteen

The day came when I didn't make it into the studio on time because the counting had become so debilitating. Why? For the life of me, I couldn't find a fifteen.

I rushed in late, breathing heavily, tore off my running shoes and helplessly tried to verbalize what I needed to in front of the mic. The script handed to me by my resentful producer lay in front of me, that sheaf of paper feeling not so different from the one given to me by the doctor in the ER months earlier.

At the end of the show, I walked straight up to Don's desk. "I need to talk to you," I said.

Don didn't even look up. "Drink in an hour?"

I puttered at my desk, then we headed over to Chill Winston. I was feeling anything but chill. I didn't say anything until our requisite rosé and beer were plunked on the table. I took a nervous gulp and said plainly, "I need to stop."

"Stop what?"

"The daily show. It's getting to me. I just don't think I can do it anymore."

Don looked at me as if seeing me for the first time. I had heard only sparse details about the passing of his daughter — a young woman with bright red hair and a captivating smile. A woman so remarkably vibrant and alive that everyone commented upon it, even strangers.

I wondered what Don was seeing as he looked at me, but I knew what I saw in the mirror: a person whose spirit was deadened, trammelled by the mechanistic purity of grief.

"What do you want to do?" he said, not unkindly.

I looked down at my half-empty wineglass and picked at my cuticles. "I'm not sure," I stammered.

But I realized I was lying. There was something I wanted to do.

I was tired of interviewing — of the standardized process of question-answer, with me guiding it all as if I were steering a ship, as if I held the golden legend to the map. I was a lousy cartographer, the grief told me so. I couldn't read the map anymore. Something had to change. I didn't have the answers, and I didn't have the questions any longer.

But . . . I'd been thinking for a while about the acknowledgements in books and how each acknowledgement tells a story. I've devoured the acknowledgements of every book I've ever picked up, and I wondered about the lifelines connecting the author to the person being acknowledged. Sometimes I've traced them like literary bread crumbs, following them from one book to another, noticing the radical reciprocity between writers who acknowledge each other.

I had wondered about seemingly innocuous acknowledgements, the cryptic ones that hold within them private jokes. Before each interview, I combed through each author's acknowledgements, wondering what role each person played in making that book come to life.

I'd always wanted to hear the story behind the story. I saw my chance now.

"I think what I want to do is a show where I invite a writer on, ask them why they acknowledged a certain person in their book, then invite that person on — and put them in conversation." I took another sip and said, with a little more courage, "And then I just get out of the way and let them talk to each other."

"So you basically want to ask people why they care for one another?" He looked at me as if I was crazy, and maybe I was, a little. But I was also not wrong, I didn't think. And he wasn't wrong either. "You really want to do this?" he said. "You're just going to replace one show for another?"

I said, "Yes, I can't do the daily anymore. I think I want this to be a weekly show." And with that statement, I felt the weight of the past few months float above me. I saw how the freight of it all had always been too much, but I hadn't known it.

"Fine. I think we can do that. When would you want to start?"

"Um," I said, "next week?"

Don looked at me with shock, and I could see him trying to figure out who would sub in once I was gone, for the short term and for the long term. A different kind of arithmetic. But this math was not my concern.

On my way home, I didn't count at all.

Well, almost not at all.

Surah Yaseen

Do you know about the power of Thursdays?

We knew not to disturb her on Thursday nights, between eight and nine. Her bedroom door slightly ajar, as a child I would peer in to catch a glimpse of her in her worn-out paisley hijab, a safety pin under her chin holding the threadbare fabric together. It had been her mother's, and her grandmother's before that. When it became mine, decades later, it dissolved in my hands.

She would kneel on her prayer mat, a silver thali in front of her. It held but a few almonds, a couple slices of McIntosh apple, a stainless-steel cup of water in the middle.

She was reading Surah Yaseen, a prayer for the dead. Like clockwork, she read the prayer every week for her mother, her father, her grandmother, all those who had passed before her.

We knew better than to bother her on Thursday nights. If I did dare go into her bedroom, my wide eyes expectant, wanting to know where my misplaced piano book was, or a beloved toy, she would turn her gaze on me and crescendo the volume of her recitation, louder and louder, shooing me out of the room with her hands.

"*Illaa rahmatam minnaa wa mataa'an ilaa heen . . .*"

Afterwards, she'd search me out, gripping the plate in one hand, the glass in the other.

"Aww, Mom!" I'd complain, as she popped the almonds into my mouth and Ray's, cajoling us into eating them, the grains of salt tantalizing our tongues.

"Stop it!" we'd cry, as she held the glass to our lips.

"Please, *beti*," she'd say, an entreating look on her face. "It's the blessed water."

Eating these blessed fruits, drinking the blessed water, would apparently protect us.

Recently, I learned online that there are many benefits to reading Yaseen:

Our very dear prophet Mohammed said: "Whoever recited
Yaseen during the night seeking the approval of Allah,
Allah would forgive him . . . [when] a person recites Yaseen
with pure and sincere intentions to gratify Allah during the
night, then he will wake up free from sin after the morning.
Later, if a believer makes sure to recite Yaseen before going
to bed only to gain the pleasure of Allah Almighty, then he
must be confident that his sins are forgiven while he sleeps."

I also read in *Sunan Abi Dawud* to "Recite Yaseen on those who die."

When she first became sick, she gave me a prayer book identical to hers. In it, she had inscribed:

For my Cherished Child Minelle,
May these "surahs" from the Quran fill your heart and soul
with Peace and Joy forever. I have been blessed a million
blessings to have been presented this gift from God. YOU —
my Daughter, my Friend, my Angel. xxx MOM.

On the next page, the table of contents. Circled in black, *Yaa Seen*, and below it, she'd written:

Every Thursday for loved ones who have passed away. Place
a glass of water and a small plate of fruits, 3 or 4 almonds,

nuts, etc. and a few strawberries or *any kind of fruit*. Then eat and drink with family.

I didn't pay a lot of attention to this wish when she was alive. But she doesn't ask for much, even in death. So I do it now. Every Thursday, I sit on the floor, reading Yaseen. My mind often wanders as I try to focus on the sacred text. Of course, I don't read Arabic. Does it matter? Maybe all that matters is that I do it.

I don't miss a Thursday. The nuts, the apple in front of me now. My partner, an atheist, takes an almond off the CorningWare plate we inherited from his mother without a word. Cole munches on the apple contently. No one complains.

Sometimes some water is left in the Riedel crystal glass, so I leave it on my dresser overnight in front of the framed snapshot of my mom and me at my cousin's wedding in Washington. Me in a yellow chiffon dress, her in a scarlet silk sheath populated with flowers. We are both laughing at something in the distance, our mouths gaping. I take a sip from this glass when I get dressed on Friday morning.

I look up the word *rotation* and find this on Dictionary.com: "The movement or path of the earth or a heavenly body turning on its axis . . . one complete turn of such a body . . . regularly recurring succession."

This rotation, perhaps, a small revolution of sorts for me.

PART SIX

DEATH IS NOT
THE OPPOSITE OF LIFE

"Death is not the opposite of life, but a part of it."

— HARUKI MURAKAMI, *Blind Willow, Sleeping Women*

What I Remember
When I Really Try to Listen

Now that we've exchanged intimacies, I think I might be ready to tell you what I wasn't before.

You know — about how she sounded.

Her girlish giggle as we shared a crackling chocolate-and-vanilla-cream-filled millefeuille in that cozy café in Paris. The gentle, instructive tone she used with her Montessori students as she helped them build their pink tower. "*Mashallah*, beautiful work!" The cadence of her Iranian accent, the sound of her long vowels, the way she said *vitamins* with a slightly British intonation, influenced by her many years of living in London. Hell, I even miss the sound of her brutish bellow as she screamed at me for not doing something she wanted me to do: not marrying the man she wanted me to marry, not studying what she wanted me to study. "*Beti*, why can't you just work a little harder?" I think she said.

I remember the way it felt to hear her voice — to be bathed in her honeyed tones as she sang to me as a child, the way she murmured what I think might have been "I love you" in Farsi, burying her face in my long dark hair.

I don't remember exactly what she said. But I know I miss how she said it.

Stray Sentences

As a non-white woman, continually taunted with racial slurs, and forced to sit silent in spaces of danger where speaking would render me too vulnerable, I have learned to stay quiet. I used to think the opposite of silence is speech. It sounds true enough. But now, now with her gone, I know better. Now I know that silence is deafeningly loud, and strong, and true and real and vital and can holler at you until your head aches with the sadness of it all. That the silence can envelope you, and smother you with its screams if only you would pay attention.

I think now about all the times she was silenced — how it was not just tongue cancer that rendered her mute, but the many, many years of staying silent and not telling her story, not speaking up, not feeling safe enough to do so. I think about the impact of being torn from her family when she was merely a toddler, kept away from her mother at such a delicate age. What did that do to her voice? And is that what made her so stubbornly committed to giving me mine?

Since she has gone, I have thought that without her voice in my world, I would never have the chance to hear her again. But of course, I hear her everywhere now. That is what surprised me the most. Maybe that sounds strange to you, but it is true. She is louder to me now than she was in the real world, whatever that is. Now I hear her in the sound of my son's laughter, through expressions she used to utter suddenly coming out of my mouth when I least expect them.

The shock of her words dropping from my lips.

Voicemails

Do you save voicemails?

I do. I saved hers.

Before she was diagnosed, I used to erase all her voicemails, most of the time before even listening to them. They would always start with "Muni" or "Minoushka," her pet names for me. If I was feeling generous, I might listen to the first few words. But I would never have the patience to listen to more.

But after she got sick, I kept every new voicemail safe — the ones that she left, again and again, just to say hi.

Do you remember many moons ago when "I Just Called to Say I Love You" came out? Yes, that song. I must have been twelve, thirteen. She called me at the house from her school one day and started crooning the Stevie Wonder hit as soon as I picked up. She put her all into it, pausing between "called" and "to say," lingering on "love." She always had a beautiful singing voice.

My face reddens when I think now about how I cut her off, mid-stanza, impatiently blowing my breath out loudly between my cheeks, rolling my eyes, telling her down the phone line she was being ridiculous. I suppose she was used to my callous cruelty at that point, and yet she never stopped telling me, in so many ways, how much she loved me.

I hate my old cellphone and wish I could get rid of it. But I can't, because it holds 427 messages on it, most of which I've never heard.

I can't bear to listen to them, because some of them are garbled messages from late in her illness, when it sounded like she had a handful of marbles in her mouth. But I also can't bear to delete them.

I was shopping at a grocery store in Vancouver shortly after her death. The ancient Neil Diamond song "Heartlight" came on. It's a schmaltzy, silly song of the early 1980s. My mom loved it though. She bought the tape and would sing along to it as she tidied the house, picking up dishtowels, plates from the table. An idle accompaniment to her cleanup. In the grocery store that day, my face was strewn with sudden tears.

I remembered calling CHFI-FM radio station when I was eleven or so, asking the DJ to play it, to dedicate the song to her. My voice shaky as I spoke to him.

He said, "You're adorable!"

Do you remember that moment, Mom, when the DJ came on and said excitedly, the sound crackly on the Panasonic clock radio, "Now, this one's for you, Freida! Hope I got that right, that name there, hard to pronounce that one! Well, anyway, this one's for you, Mom, from your darling daughter, Michelle!"

You were standing by your vanity cabinet. You spun around and gave me a luminous smile.

Are we good now, Mom? Do you forgive me? One song for another?

Because I still don't forgive myself. I won't. No song in the world will do that.

Storytelling

I kept wondering why I was drawn back to the course readings from my old classes, even though I was no longer teaching. Maybe it's because I looked at them differently, living theory in an entirely different way. This became clearer for me when I came across an article by the historian Joan Wallach Scott. Her son is A.O. Scott, who was at the time the film critic for the *New York Times*. I was trying desperately to book an interview with them together.

Starting to work on *Acknowledgements* made me feel more at ease. Not just because I'd gone from working on a daily show to a weekly show — although there was that. Bruce told me I didn't look so exhausted, and friends told me I seemed more relaxed. *Acknowledgements* helped me realize that no story is a solo production. It became another way of shattering the binaries that have ruled my life. Whenever I saw a daughter acknowledge a mother, I wanted to book them together on the show. I wanted to memorialize these patterns among family members, the intimate dynamics of a laugh shared between a mother and a son, of a husband affectionately speaking to his wife — and to speak not to the binaries but to that unspoken space between them.

After I wrote my plaintive letter to Joan Scott, asking her to come on the show, she turned me down but nicely. I thought about why I wanted to speak to her so badly. It was not only that I wanted to capture the dynamics between her and her son. It came back to a piece she'd written about storytelling.

Scott states that storytelling is the art of repeating stories: "It is those stories that give us insight not just into the particularities of historical experience, but also into the very meaning of the human." This is the part I really love: "For the historian to ignore the stories themselves — their form and content — is to deny agency to historical subjects, to overlook the choices they made and the ways they found to explain their actions to themselves and others."

Offering agency to historical subjects. I like this a lot: it seems to speak to the stories of those who have long gone, those who have been lost to us because of death, despair, misunderstandings, conflict. How the choices we made, continue to make, influence the choices we make now. I'd never thought about this before, but I saw now that the stories I listened to every day on the show offered context to my own life, helped me read and react to my own story differently.

Are radio hosts actually historians documenting the quotidian nature of the lives of those who have stories to share? What agency do we offer through the gift of a question? In telling stories, is it possible to create an infinitesimal space where we and others can embroider the joy, serendipity and gorgeous texture of life onto the trauma, cruelty and pain of the world? Does this mending allow for intergenerational trauma to splinter, like warm air entering the patterned cracks of ice on a bright blue lake to shatter it?

The Line between the
Surface of the Earth and the World

Mama, what is Heaven like?

It's like we are underground right now, junam. *Under the surface of the earth. It's mostly darkness. Heavy loam. Seedlings, though, hold the promise of something better.*

But, Mama, isn't it good here too?

It is, Cole, it is. But there is something better that we can imagine. When we die, we speak to the surface. We blossom. Remember, junam, *we have no idea what's on the other side of the earth, because we aren't there yet. We can only see glimmers.*

My mom, she showed me the glimmers.

(When I put this into a voice memo, glimmers comes out as *scores.*)

Remember, I hear her whisper to me. *Remember,* junam.

The Garage Sale

Shortly after I started *Acknowledgements*, I put on my favourite shirt — that white linen shirt I wore for the Gopnik interview — and shiny black tights. My feather necklace swung from my neck. I felt smart and happy and new. Blossoms and bursting green leaves were dappling the streets with warm light. It was spring in Vancouver, and the world was fresh and joyful.

I spotted a sign for a moving sale and meandered over. I told you my mom and I loved a market, and the same was true of garage sales. Sitting on stools behind a table bursting with knick-knacks were two young people, big smiles on their faces. I sifted through some books for sale in a woven basket and found some of my favourites: Jack Halberstam's *Trans**, Carmen Maria Machado's *Her Body and Other Parties*. I knew these young adults now, having seen what they'd read — *tell me what you love, and I will tell you who you are*. I liked them already. They were selling their handsomely handmade pottery — big, beautiful, glazed blue bowls that glistened in the spring sunshine.

I inspected them all idly, admiring the work, and asked them where they were moving.

They said, "We're moving to the farthest place we can think of! Newfoundland!"

I started to clap, perhaps a little too energetically; Vancouver still didn't feel like home to me. I would have given anything to get out of this city and still would.

I congratulated them. The young woman, who sported light blue curls and a crop top, cried, "We can't wait. It's going to be such an adventure!"

Nearby, a woman around my age hugged one of the large blue bowls close to her chest and smiled sadly.

I said, "You really love that bowl, don't you?"

She held on to it as if for dear life.

"What if I want it?" I said, my eyes dancing. It is meant as a joke. But I could see she took me seriously.

"I can't let go of this bowl. I'm going to buy it," she said. "You can't have it!"

"You should buy it! It's beautiful!"

Then she said, as if I hadn't said anything, "I am going to buy everything. Everything." She said this last part defiantly. But I could also hear her voice laced with something else. Lament?

The blue-haired young woman rolled her eyes. "Mom, stop it! You can't buy it all!"

The older woman looked dejected but determined. "I'm going to buy everything," she said. "My baby is leaving me. I am going to buy everything she has, so I can keep holding on to everything that is hers, everything she has touched, everything she has made — even after she goes."

I blurted out, "Good for you! I love that you're doing this! You're a good mom!"

The young woman grimaced. "Oh, Mom! You're making too big a deal out of this! We have to move!"

But the mother (now that I knew she was the mother) and I exchanged glances that said everything. I knew what she was feeling. I have felt just the same but its opposite.

She was missing her daughter, who hadn't yet left. And I was missing my mother, who had long gone.

Goodwill

After my father died, I discovered his collection of fine cotton hand-kerchiefs in the top drawer of his dresser, all of them perfectly ironed and folded, soft as a kitten's ear from repeated use over the years. I decided to keep every single one. I was ruthless on other things though: beautiful maroon gabardine suits, leather-bound books, all stuffed into a U-Haul and dragged unsentimentally to the Goodwill at the corner of Wellesley and Parliament.

I remember feeling victorious, clean, satisfied.

The next day, though, when dawn broke, I awoke with a start. I rushed to the same Goodwill at six a.m., waiting hours for the employees to open the store. The pigeons clamoured around me, loudly cooing on the dirty sidewalk where I'd plunked myself. As soon as an employee arrived and removed the steel chain from the doors, I rushed inside as if I were in a race with an unknown spirit. I bought back most of the things I'd given away the day before: heavy wooden placemats, cracked egg holders, some old cutlery. I gathered them to my chest just like the woman would at the garage sale, many years later. The register racked up the growing cost.

As I stood at the cash, I saw, out of the corner of my eye, two frat boys appraising my dad's beloved peacock taffeta sofa. Well, I wasn't sure they were frat boys, but they sure looked like it. I guess I wasn't feeling generous that day. The frat boys started to carry the sofa out. They handled it carelessly, guffawing as they left the store, almost dropping it a few times. I fought the urge to buy it back. *Don't you know who used to own that sofa? Treat it with more respect!* I could see the gentle indentation in the cushion where my dad used to sit, the mark of his strong, solid back from leaning on it, the back I'd leaned on for so many years. I yearned to sit there, to feel the space left by his shoulders one more time.

A decade later, I rummaged through the storage locker where my dad's possessions were housed. My mother's things now commingled with his stuff, in ways they never had in life. In a beat-up cardboard box, simply labelled "Goodwill," I found the items I'd bought back that day. I spilled them out on the ground and slowly sifted through the motley collection. I spotted Simone's rhinestone collar, the cracked egg cups, the placemats and all the cutlery. My grief suffocated the objects left behind.

Mother and Father as Opposites

I always thought there were miles and miles between the opposites that have guided my life. Remember them? Indian/Iranian; Hindu/ Muslim. But now I know this is not true. That I lived an illusion in thinking about these pairs as opposites. I no longer think it is about two things, two discreet entities bumping up against each other, causing friction and tension and ultimately despair. I have always been able to see the violence in these pairings — a clash that was inevitable, impossible to avoid. But without her in my life, the way I approach addition and subtraction, multiplication and division has completely changed. The arithmetic of death makes it plain to me: she is gone, he is gone, and the balance has shifted. Two minus two equals zero. *You're an orphan now, honey.* But we all lose our parents, so that can't be enough.

What I want to understand is why I keep diametrically opposed photos of them next to my bed: never a photo of them together in one place, but separate photos of them taken when they were far apart from one another, in their own orbital geographies. I see now that a half and a half don't make a whole, the phrase *significant other* a problematic one for me, just like the phrase *my better half.* Were you previously half a person?

A line from Surah Yaseen goes: "Glory be to the One who has created all things in pairs — be it what the earth produces, their genders, or what they do not know." I keep getting stuck on that line.

Before I used to think it meant pairs as sacred things. Now I think that it is referring to the space between the pair that holds the most reverent knowledge. In the wresting apart of pairs lies the wisdom. Of course, there are many interpretations, but this is mine.

I think now about question and answer. Are they opposites? I had conceptualized my parents as opposites, but maybe they weren't. I had assumed that they were, a way of telling my own little story about myself. But maybe I made her my opposite. Which was also not true. I relied too much on the idea that being half of her would make me whole. A half and a half do not make a whole — that whole I will never be. I had relied on that comfortable ease of the pairing of mother/daughter only to have it wrenched out from under me. My reliance on that binary lasted for far too long to make a whole.

Now I am only daughter. Is that enough?

Perugia

I was invited to speak in Perugia, Italy, at an international journalism conference. In some ways, this wasn't unusual. I had been a journalism professor before I took on the radio job. I was used to conferences. But now I was being asked to speak about the radio show instead of presenting research I'd done. I liked the change.

I was also becoming quietly proud of the work we were doing on *Acknowledgements*. Nearly a year had passed since I'd made the switch, and something surprising was happening: I felt a lot less alone doing this particular show. It was no longer only me and a guest. I didn't have to pry the story out of one person in the same way, with the same intensity. I was relishing the companionship of a trio: me in conversation with two others who clearly cared about one another and were eager to showcase each other's spirits. I got to bear witness to all sorts of affection and love. I was privy to intimacies and had the great gift of sharing those intimacies with listeners. I saw this in the conversations I had with writers like Jessica J. Lee and her former advisor, Dr. Cate Sandilands; in the space shared between Heidi Sopinka, author of *The Dictionary of Animal Languages* and the friend she acknowledged, the writer Claire Cameron. Between Sharon Bala and Lisa Moore. Jan Wong and her son, Sam Schulman. Carol Off and Naomi Duguid.

When I landed in Perugia, the place was teeming with journalists and academics. Google and Facebook had set up tables. If you spoke with them, you got a free latte. I lingered at their stations for a while, listening to their patter while I sipped my coffee.

I was slated to speak with other women journalists of colour on a panel entitled "Her Story: Are We Giving Non-white Women Journalists Enough Agency to Report on the Stories They Believe In?" When I arrived at the room where the session would be held, there was a sign on the door: *Session cancelled*. One of the presenters had her missed flight, so the session had been moved to a taped one, two hours from then on the rooftop of the conference hotel.

The rooftop offered an astonishingly gorgeous view of Perugia: the rusty iron roofs, the rolling hills, the mustard-coloured landscapes. To better remember that day, I've watched the tape of that talk a few times. I can see now how different I looked from when my mother was sick. My hair was shorn short, a crime I'd committed almost immediately after she died, ordering the hairstylist to cut it all off. But the colour was back in my cheeks. Only someone who knew me really well would have known how much I was still grieving.

In the session, Hani, the organizer, mentioned something about her favourite food. I'm not sure why this came up, it was unusual for a panel conversation, but then again this was a session about our stories.

"I have grown up on a Burmese dish called *khao-swe*," she said. "I'm actually writing a book about it because my mother introduced me to it."

I was taken aback, astonished. "That's my favourite food, too — my mother introduced it to me as well!"

We chuckled over this coincidence, and I made a mental note to talk about it later with Hani. The next morning over freshly squeezed orange juice, pastries and cold cuts, we enthused over the odd serendipity.

"How is it possible that you and me, coming from such different worlds, share this thing in common?" Hani said. I shook my head, not able to answer in words but also knowing the reason: the way that food travels, the way that meals speak to us, bring us together. The geography of taste.

For years after, Hani dropped me a short note from time to time to share with me a new tidbit about her book on *khao-swe* — how the meal had touched many people around the world and how it affects people so strongly. I recalled, too, a man I had met in London in my twenties with whom I fell hopelessly in love, a saxophone player from Perth, who told me upon our first meeting that his favourite dish was *khao-swe*, because his best friend's mother made it for him.

These little moments, not so little, that bind us to each other.

On the flight home to Vancouver, I prepped interviews for the week. I had two memoirs to finish reading. As the plane rumbled to a halt on the runway, I surreptitiously checked my email; we hadn't been told we could turn our phones on yet. I'd just been thinking, *I have the best job in the world.*

There was a note from Don. It was one line with an attachment: "Sorry to have to tell you this." The attachment was on letterhead and read:

TO: Minelle Mahtani

Due to ongoing financial difficulties, and further to today's all staff meeting, this notice will confirm that your services will no longer be required at Roundhouse Radio after April 30, 2018.

This is in no way a reflection of your work on *Sense of Place* or *Acknowledgements* — or your other contributions to Roundhouse Radio. I will do all that I can to help you in your future endeavours.

My heartfelt apologies and gratitude,
Don

I was in disbelief. We'd all talked about the station going under for so long that I'd stopped believing it might actually happen. I could hear the flight attendant across the aisle asking me to put my phone away, but I texted Don, "Is it only me?" Given my show was a bit of an oddity, I assumed I would be among the first to go. There had been a spate of firings at Roundhouse already, but my show had been spared. I had hardly finished typing the words when I caught the flight attendant glowering. I dropped my phone in the pocket of the seat in front of me, and that's when it rang.

I fished it out — it was Don. Before I could get a word out, he said sternly, "Yep. Just you." He waited a beat, then chuckled. "No, no, it's everyone!" he said, now laughing uproariously. "Why would you assume it would just be you? The whole station is going under!"

And I started to laugh. At the absurdity of it all, my own ego-centrism and the idea that it was somehow better that it was all of us, and not just me. My chuckle grew into a guffaw, then into large snorts until I was howling, just as I had on the day of my mother's death and of her memorial.

Last Day on Air

The next few weeks were heavy and surreal. Walking into the office was like heading into a cemetery. We were all bustling about, but we knew what was coming. Day after day, I noticed fewer and fewer people at their desks. The tabletops were no longer scattered with advanced reading copies from publishers, no more leftover scripts, no errant ballpoint pens. Instead, they were scrubbed clean. People were exiting the place, getting their pink slips, saying quiet goodbyes.

My last show. I had specifically scheduled it to be an episode about a memoir by Natalie Appleton titled *I Have Something to Tell You*. The book is about beginnings and endings: a story about how on the eve of Christmas and getting a proposal from a man she wasn't sure she wanted to marry, Natalie abandoned her life in Medicine Hat, Alberta, for Bangkok. The book is about taking a leap of faith. I called it "a grittier *Eat, Pray, Love*" in my intro.

In the acknowledgements, Natalie thanked her aunt Cindy. In an initial call with Natalie, she told me, "[Cindy] helped me find my home." That was all I needed to know to book them — to put them into conversation.

I began the show, as I did every episode of *Acknowledgements*, with the question "Why do you acknowledge the person on the other side of the phone line?"

"Because Cindy played such a big role in my life, and she was so wonderful about just letting me sound off to her," Natalie said. She sounded like she was beaming. "I would get to venture into her warm and cozy little world, and she would just make me feel better a lot. She really sistered me through that time in my life."

"Cindy, I have to bring you in here. Do you remember that moment vividly in Natalie's life when she came to be with you? How hard was it for you to hear those kinds of stories? What was . . . where was Natalie at, do you think, at that point in her life?"

Cindy said, "Oh, it was definitely hard to hear. You want to be there to give them the advice to walk them through, and in your heart you know, as her aunt, when she has to take the steps to get there and . . . and you hope and pray that . . . that she sees that. And just with a little bit of guidance and love and a grilled cheese sandwich . . . It's just being supportive. When I look at her at that period of time, you can tell, she knew she needed to be somewhere else and needed just to find where that would be. And to take the time to find that right spot."

The love between them threaded throughout the entire interview. In returning to it now, what strikes me is that deep nested care, the joy shared between them. It was in every syllable, the heartbeat of every word. I could hear Cindy breathing when I asked her if Natalie's story made her believe in magic. *What made me ask that?* And Cindy's voice breaking, rife with tears, when she replied, "Yes, I do. I believe that Natalie was truly being guided. It's like she left home to find home."

I asked Natalie the same question. She took a beat before saying, "I often had a sense of overwhelming warmth and feeling that I was going the right way. The right doors seemed to be opening up, and if I was trusting in that, I would be okay. People call that different things — intuition, ways of knowing — but if you think about the mere odds of me meeting my [husband] thousands of miles away from where we grew up, it makes me feel that our family members who are not near us play a role. I love the idea of those people doing some magic for us up there."

The last question I asked before I walked out of the studio forever was focused on endings. "I have one last question for you, Natalie. It's the line that comes at the end of the book that dissolved me in tears. It's two words. It's 'please listen.'"

"Yeah." I heard Natalie take a deep breath. "Once I realized the title that I wanted to use, then it was like, *But what is that something that I have to tell you?* The strongest message that I wanted to share was that you will get feelings or signs or experiences — maybe just nudges from the world that are trying to open your eyes to a path toward something that's going to make you happy, and you can choose to see and follow those nudges or not."

"Well, I think for a lot of our listeners, this book will really open up a space for them to trust in that inner voice and take that leap of faith. Maybe it means to get out of a bad relationship or to go to a new place. And just as if . . . just the way that you encourage your sons to think about taking that leap of faith, I think our listeners will hopefully do the same. I want to thank both of you for a beautiful conversation. Thank you."

When the board operator hit the "end record" button, Natalie and Cindy told me how special it was to have that conversation and said that I was a great interviewer. I still couldn't hear the praise but for different reasons now.

I feel so fortunate that that was how I signed off for the last time.

It would be years before I returned to this interview. When I did, there was the inevitable cringe of hearing my voice, the ticks that still irritate me so. But I also see now how there was a message for me within it. At the time of the recording, I thought it was a beautiful conversation about digging your way out of a hole, about travelling to find yourself, about listening to your inner knowing. But I now know it was about something else, too — about how the pairing of Cindy and Natalie and their abundant love was a mirror for the love I had with my mother. That perhaps in some small way, my mother was speaking to me through this interview — encouraging me to listen to the signs.

I understood during that last interview that I didn't always need to speak loudly to make my voice heard. By stepping out of the way, making space for others, a different and wiser voice emerged. *Acknowledgements* helped me see that I could create a constellation of connections, and in the power of those connections was a braided thread of stars, shining brightly, and a symphony of sound.

The Thing You Cannot Say

I am going to say the thing you can't say. Or the thing I want to say but never felt like I could utter. These words are the worst, most despicable words I could share.

Can I say them to you?

I am glad she is gone.

Are you surprised I am saying this?

I am glad she is gone not only because she is out of pain — although, of course, it is mostly that.

I am glad she is gone because her death was not just an ending but a new beginning for me, a beginning of a new kind of relationship with her. A relationship in which I could revisit my connection with her on my own terms. Although she held the spiritual connective thread of our tenuous relationship in her hands, her grip, I could, in this world, revisit my own thinking about her, who she was, what she did, why she had such a hold on me.

Is this where I tell you that, of course, I miss her and, of course, I want her back?

Yes, that's true.

And the opposite can be true, too, all at once.

That I miss her every day, and that I appreciate this new way of being alongside her, being near and without her too.

Questions (Again)

I realize now that it's not just about the questions we ask. My demand for answers — *Where are you? What are you doing?* and my all-time personal favourite *Why did you leave me?* — was about my refusal to really listen.

I know now that I didn't listen to what she didn't say. I will never know how she got that tiny scar on her right baby finger. I think she told me once, but I don't remember. I will never hear her utter the histories of my ancestors to me, never learn the names of the faces in her old photo albums. With youthful indifference, I had brushed away her memories.

I had thought I was well acquainted with the strength of silence, learning how to hold my tongue, meticulously manipulating when to speak and when to be quiet. But it turns out I don't know a damned thing about silence. Now I know the pain and the power of that absence. No longer hearing my mother's voice, I have learned what silence can be.

Her Last Words

When I eventually finished packing up her things, I found what I couldn't have dared to hope for. One of her old journals. As if the orange folder and the poem weren't enough.

The journal was threadbare, a maroon religious journal with daily texts on the bottom of every page. It looked a little like the dictionary I had balanced on my head all those years earlier. The cover was embossed with the words *Daily Help Yearbook*. It mostly chronicled the year she was twenty-two.

My mom was writing in it after her own mother had perished in a fire in their home, a cigarette butt found hanging from her fingertips. My mother was the one charged with identifying the charred body.

On some level, I felt it wasn't my place to read this journal, this deeply private place that held her secret revelations. But I opened it anyway, and the pages fell easily to one entry, from May 1962. My mother wrote, in her beautiful cursive hand, this letter to her mother:

My dearest, and most under-appreciated Maman,

My friend Salim and I were listening to a tape on his tape
recorder, and he put on all we had recorded in Abadan
together. You don't know what happened to me when
I heard your magnetic, striving, forceful, intensely pained
voice — I cried, and could not stop!

I am still aching.

Maman, my closest Love, I did not realize how indispensable
you are to me! I did not even think I could love anyone so
much, was capable of so much love, now I know, oh! How
fathomless and how infinite is my love for you.

Dearest Mother, to be most open, I cannot live without you
and your presence. I merely exist, pass from day to day, like
a blurred shadow, but now that you are away, I treasure your
Divine Love.

Maman, I need you, Maman, please pray for me. Please don't
desert me. I need to hear your controlled voice, which speaks
without the need of definite words. How much you have
suffered! You are a woman, a symbol of human experience,
and you decided to write an unforgettable story. You were
the book. The story that painfully emotionally reflected
what your life so wished to express.

You were the book, the story.
Just as she was, for me.
I don't know all her stories, that is true. Some will forever remain
out of reach to me. But I can speak some of her stories into exis-
tence now.
It's hard for me not to see her yearning for her mother's voice as
parallel to my own, our distinct revolutions overlapping. The revolving nature of intergenerational grief.

Radio as
Emotional One-Night Stands

How do I feel about interviewing now?

I now see radio as a series of emotional one-night stands. I became closer to the people I interviewed than to my kin. The conversations with strangers became intimate so fast, like falling with abandon down a rabbit hole. I longed to hear what inspired them, what made them who they are. Those seeds planted, like the placenta in the earth. Intimacy, planted and delicately watered.

The sacred before and after the interview. Those exquisite moments at the coffee machine, where I'd offer them something warm to drink, their hands enveloping our chipped Roundhouse Radio mugs. The way those lost moments bookended the story they shared with me.

I'm embarrassed to tell you that in the early months after the show ended, I was irrationally angry. I realized it was because I'd become accustomed to a daily pattern of sanctioned yet unsurveilled intimacy. I could ask hard, painful, pointed questions. And it would all be okay as long as I handled it right. I couldn't do that in my real life. I was too timid to try. I would have loved to ask an old friend from dance class why she had been so passive-aggressive toward me, to ask my brother why he uses sarcastic jokes to hide the pain of our childhoods. But I couldn't ask those questions to those I was supposed to be most intimate. With strangers, it's totally fine to do that. Why is it fine? In the sacred space of the studio, I could ask strangers emotionally sanctioned questions that leave people unsettled.

I still can't do this with my loved ones.

Questions (Yes, Again)

I listened to an interview with the singer Ani DiFranco a little while back. She said that when her memoir came out, every interview she did felt like a public exorcism. *Exorcism.* That stayed with me: how taxing each interview exchange must have been for her. I think about how so many writers get asked the same questions again and again on book tours — that extraction like dental surgery. And yet I can't forget that moment when I tweeted something like, "We never get the author in the interview — only the person who wrote the story," and some of the writers I'd interviewed retweeted it, a kind of affirmation that maybe I was right.

It's been said that the best interview sounds like a conversation. I'm no longer convinced of this. I am no longer convinced because *conversation* assumes two people listen to each other with similar levels of respect, dignity, space for responses. Lately I've been thinking, *What if the best conversations sound like interviews?* I say this because I now sit, day after day, in stifling rooms at the university, watching faculty struggle to make small talk as they grab their coffees. Too many of us are unable to speak about matters that really matter to us: our sick child at home, our parents' deterioration. Of course, there's no space for this talk in the workplace. But what if there were? What would that look like?

I know that I am a junkie for the intimate interview. I can't get that pleasure anywhere else, really. Those emotional one-night stands.

I saw this most plainly and painfully play out when a few of us at the university got together for prosecco one afternoon — a deliberate attempt to inject some joy into our shrouded workdays. We met on my colleague and friend Shirley's sunny patio; on her table sat an inviting spread of sundried tomatoes she'd made herself slathered in glistening olive oil and nestled with homemade hummus, freshly torn basil and roasted pine nuts. The food was luscious; the conversation was not. It was as stifled as the air in a conference room at an academic conference, tight like the vestibule I was in years ago.

Something was off.

It was in the way we were relating. The talk remained shallow, discreet — a little nervous laughter, with interjections to complain about work. But I was done with all this. I had spent years asking writers why they think the way they do, why they take the risk to share their stories with us. Stupidly perhaps, I wanted to ask these colleagues why they do the work they do, what inspires them and what shapes their lives.

So I took a deep breath and asked why they love who they love. Inappropriate, yes, but the prosecco, bubbling away gently in a bright shapely flute, inspired me to take the risk. And they opened up slowly, like a shard of light blooming on a pine kitchen table. The conversation shifted, first slightly, then significantly. We discovered that two of us share strangely similar meet-cutes with our partners. I was surprised but not shocked at this discovery and was very glad to have made it. The laughter that ensued felt honest, true.

I see now that for me, conversations will never be the same if I just allow myself to take the risk of asking different questions.

Tombstones

With the radio station shutting down, I had to look for new work. I was desperate to find an academic job after so much time away from teaching. I missed my life as a professor. I wished I had thought more carefully about what it would take to move to another university, but with great hubris I'd thought it would be easy.

There was a position open to become head of a journalism school in Toronto. I applied, in part because I knew they would most likely offer Bruce a position, too, if I got it — unlike my former university job in Toronto, which had necessitated my move to Vancouver in the first place. I made it through the first interview, but in the second round, it became obvious that the position wasn't going to be seen as right for me. I felt strange being asked questions after a few years of asking them. I was rusty in answering, and the questions were odd and unwieldy.

The question that really bothered me: "Why do you want to come back here?" As if it made no sense for me to want to return to my hometown.

But that wasn't really the question. The questions they were really asking were *Why us, why now, what is it about us that you love, and are you willing to become more like us?* Like likes like, you know.

I was infuriated by the question, heat rising from beneath my ivory silk top. Instead of offering them the response I knew they pined for, the insipid, thin, carefully curated answer — *Your school is the best*

in the country, so there's no doubt in my mind I would want to teach here —
I instead blurted out a very wrong answer.

"I want to live in the same city where my mother is buried."

This answer surprised me. What had unearthed that vociferous answer from my larynx with such force that day? I could see that the committee members were equally surprised by my unconventional response. The only serene and unflappable face: the sole Indigenous member of the committee. *Oh, thank you for telling me who you really are,* I thought his eyes said. Maybe I imagined it.

But what I know I did not imagine: the shock registering over the other committee members' faces when they realized I had abruptly changed the terms of the game from the professional to the personal; the job market, of course, is no place for such unabashedly vulnerable declarations. But it was the truth, buried deep inside me: the desire to be in closer proximity to what would have been her almost fully decayed body, covered with grass and moss. Why blurt this out to a group of steely mouthed strangers, who were adjudicating me with every perfunctory question?

Maybe I did it to bring a moment of honesty to an almost always insincere process, a process that served to be fatal for me (which I'm sure you're not surprised to learn). I knew I had said the most wrong thing I could ever say in an interview. But I also knew that the opposite was true. Something snapped into place for me during the interview: the recognition that my body, barely breathing with its own thin beliefs, wanted to be near hers, even though it was dead and lifeless.

I had made it a point not to visit her grave. I didn't trust myself to visit her, to drink in the soothing presence of a gentle leaf blowing above the willow tree bursting with life near her grave, or a blood-red tulip dusted with sun-yellow by the gravestone kitty-corner to hers, blooming like an open-throated baby bird, craving more?

Could I trust in those signs? No.

And because I felt I could not trust them, I could not bring myself to visit her at all.

I am mortified to admit that I still have not, after all these years, designed a headstone for her, that reality a cheek-staining embarrassment on the rare moments I did visit her, knowing that all the other Muslim souls surrounding her had gorgeous rose-granite engraved headstones that unabashedly declared their children's love for them. I could imagine all of the dead Muslim mothers crowding around her, clucking their tongues at her own children's disrespect: *"Baap re,"* they would say, shaking their dead heads, rolling their dead eyes, their bodies pushing the spring daffodils up through the ground, each one chastising my mother so. "What kind of children did you raise? *Astaghfirullah!"*

And her reply, a cheery "I'm sure they are getting around to it!" within the first few months of her passing, and now after six months, a resigned and exasperated *"Chutiya sala,* I raised heathens. You were right."

And she would be right.

Perhaps in some way, the refusal to craft the headstone remained a kind of cheeky rebellion against her death, a way of saying without words: *You can't possibly be gone if I don't do this for you; you can't possibly be buried in that ground if I refuse to mark it with a ritual, a sign.* And in not doing this, I am saying her death didn't really happen, that Joan Didion–infused magical thinking still so firmly implanted in my brain.

But on the day of the interview of the job I really wanted but ultimately did not get, I saw that I had to accept that she really was dead, and in that breathless blurt, my voice box knew enough to utter the truth finally: *She's gone, she's gone, she's gone.*

Still Thinking about Repair

I couldn't stop thinking about repair. I didn't think about the word in its entirety, as if such a thing was ever possible. Rather I kept returning to its parts — re-pair, as if I could possibly re-pair myself without her in my world.

Rushdie's words from our interview echoed in my mind: "I do think it's the story of human life that we are, you know, we are all beaten up by life. We all carry those bruises. Some of us to a greater degree than others, and certainly one of the great subjects of literature is how human beings deal with that."

Maybe we can't survive in wholes. Wholes are but a mirage, really. We can only survive in parts. Then I remember, again, *Was I ever only half of a person?*

The scholar Steven Jackson explains that there are gifts in broken-world thinking. I like that idea: the world is almost irrevocably broken, and what do we take away from that knowledge? This reminds me of the Japanese custom of *kintsugi* — the art of putting broken pottery pieces back together with gold — a metaphor for embracing your flaws and imperfections. Isn't that an example of broken-world thinking? The act of creating something beautiful from destruction and loss.

Can't I do that too?

Jackson says broken-world thinking allows for contemplation of breakdown, dissolution and change, rather than innovation, development and design. I like this a lot.

Maybe I need to ask: What happens when we take erosion and decay — rather than novelty, growth and progress — as our starting points in thinking through the possibilities of life after the loss of someone we love?

I don't have an answer. Not yet.

I think about how her last words to me really held no sound, just her mouthing the words "wish come true" as she drew a heart with her fingers in the air.

The poet Rumi writes, "There is a voice that doesn't use words. Listen."

PART SEVEN

JOY

"We are all one question, and the best answer seems to be love —
a connection between things."

— MARY RUEFLE, *Madness, Rack, and Honey*

Maui

In that gauzy mind-haze between grief and relief, shortly after she died, I devised a dastardly scheme — I'm so goddamned clever. I told my family I would be getting married in Maui in August. Six months almost to the day from when she died.

I notified Bruce about this arrangement. He couldn't refuse me because, you know, my mother had just died. Everyone said yes to coming, even though the costs were exorbitant, because, of course, my mother had just died. I didn't think about how manipulative this was until later. At the time, all I could think about was that I wanted my brain to be emblazoned only with joy and sand and salt and endless copper sunsets and succulent chicken skewers with charcoal ribbons that smelled divine and the sultry sounds of the ocean. A rotation of sorts, a way to make good on the bad from years ago.

Want to know what happened before?

Maui, 1996. I'd planned the lavish trip on my own. I was twenty-four years old. I booked an expensive hotel on the coast and took surfing lessons with a slim and stunning man named Colton, or some other white name. During our lesson, I fantasized that he'd fallen crazy in love with me and whisked me away for a romantic afternoon. Instead, I clumsily stumbled through the waves, and when his allotted hour with me was over, there were no overtures. He hopped in his Jeep and headed back into town alone. I stubbornly decided to master the craft on my own. A wave hit — I went one way, the board went another. The board was attached to my ankle. The board zipped through the water. I heard a snap. My shoulder had dislocated. I screamed out in pain, but no one was there to hear me. I paddled like a dog to the shore, somehow got myself into my rental car and drove myself to the nearest clinic. (Good thing I had medical insurance.) The Iranian doctor took one look at it and snapped it into place. The pain was excruciating. *There goes my holiday*, I thought. I spent the next week by the hotel pool, my arm in a cloth sling. It wasn't terrible. In fact, it was kind of terrific.

When I returned to work at the CBC after my holiday, I had a tan that was the envy of the office. A prominent television anchor uttered two words as he passed me in the hallway, the only words he would ever speak to me: "Nice tan." Another famous host, one I worked with regularly, asked about my trip and then planned the exact same one, except, as he said to me with a grin, "I won't stay at that dingy hotel you were at. Four Seasons all the way, baby!"

Maui, 2016. Tropical air enveloped us, redolent with the intoxicating smell of frangipani. My son frolicked in the waves with his cousins. I could hear his sweet taffy laughter. The rehearsal dinner that we didn't plan — twenty-five of us from far-flung places like Auckland, Toronto, Washington, New York, Montreal — all of us eating pizza that was sweating in grease, consumed along with countless bottles of Merlot that Sylvia had bought as a wedding gift at the nearby grocery store that day.

The wedding would be on Makena Beach, the very beach I'd walked on heartbroken years earlier, my shoulder in a sling. There would be no father-daughter walk to the makeshift altar for me. I was alone in the public washroom beforehand, checking my makeup in the foggy, scratched mirror. Just minutes before, I sat in the parking lot in the open back trunk of the hatchback rental car while my cousin carefully applied rouge to my cheeks. She had done a makeup test the night before at the reception, meticulously finding the right shade for me. Bringing more *ameh-biance* to the scene.

My wedding dress was from J. Crew. It had satin spaghetti straps, ivory lace. I'd ordered it in early March, a month after her death. When it arrived, it slid effortlessly over my emaciated body, loose in all the wrong places. But a few months later, when I took it to my friend Bonnie to alter it, it fit perfectly. She'd shrugged, smiled and quietly put away her needle and thread.

I opened the bathroom door, took off my Michael Kors strappy sandals and ran, ran, ran, down the grassy hill to the beach, where my mentor, cousins, best friend, son and soon-to-be husband were waiting.

The day was perfect, marring the obvious omission of Mother, Father. Just my brother, son and Bruce. No more two, a new three. A different math.

From our program:

Some Persian aspects of our ceremony: a scarf or shawl, made out of silk or any other fine fabric, is held over the bride's and bridegroom's heads during the ceremony by various happily married female relatives. Two sugar cones, otherwise known as *kalleh ghand*, made out of hardened sugar, will be used during the ceremony. These sugar cones are ground together above the bride's and bridegroom's heads during the ceremony to shower them in sugar, symbolizing sweetness and happiness.

My cousin from New York, the one who had sent me the flowers, the one I'd read the dictionary to when she was just a baby in my arms, hoping she would turn out smart (she did), had gone to so much trouble for me. She'd meticulously sourced the *kalleh ghand* from a specialty bakery online and had packed them along with spices and yards of white tulle so we could wrap the sugar loaves up like giant candies, as well as a little mirror for the ritual. Her generosity overwhelmed me, leaving me speechless.

My family held the long piece of silk above Bruce's head and mine as we dropped to our knees in the sand, and I was mesmerized back into memory. I remembered my mother, dressed in a gold-plated white sari, rubbing sugar cubes over my uncle and soon-to-be aunt at our home. I was nine. All three of them had since passed, but I could see them, feel them close. I could hear my mother's ululating, that high-pitched sound made at Islamic weddings that possesses a thrilling, trilling quality. The joy in that sound, undeniable.

Dinner at the Mill House Maui restaurant followed our beach wedding. Lush emerald-green mountains and swaying pineapple trees cocooned us. I was wearing another new outfit: a halter dress made of ivory chiffon, reminiscent of Marilyn Monroe's infamous dress from *The Seven Year Itch*. In the photos with Bruce, my leg is slightly kicked up in delight.

On the menu: sparkling brut rosé, coffee-roasted beets, fromage blanc beaded with sweat, bright marigold carrot-fennel-caraway gnocchi, wilted greens, smoked macadamia nut pesto, brown butter curd and poppy-red tuna tartare chilling on a sparkling white plate. The gnocchi, light little pillows. Four months later, an email from my cousin: "I'm still dreaming about that gnocchi."

The waitress who served us at the long family-style table was kind and welcoming. I approached her at the back of the restaurant to say a quiet thank you because I was so moved by her kindness, my cheeks surely red from the Wolfberger Brut Rosé. I spontaneously blurted out that my mom had just died. I told her I'd dragged my family to Maui to celebrate life rather than dwell in sadness. She looked solemn. But did I stop there? Of course I didn't. I rambled out something about feathers. I told her I'd seen them everywhere on this trip, that they represented my mother to me.

I felt stupid. I'd said too much.

A smile broke out on her face. She pulled out a necklace from beneath her blouse. On it, a little silver feather charm. She said, "You're not going to believe this, but my mom's dead too. For me, a feather symbolizes her spirit. It's why I always wear this around my neck."

I pulled out my silver feather necklace. Of course I was wearing it that day. We both started to laugh-cry, holding on to each other, rocking, cackling. Later that week, I returned to the restaurant, a bottle of J. Lohr Cabernet Sauvignon nestled in my bag for her. We exchanged emails and kept in touch for a while.

Everything felt so uncomplicated on the trip. The weather was perfect. Joylyn and I sat on the beach the next night near our rented apartments, our faces lit only by moonlight. Our respective families were asleep, lulled by the sounds of the shoreline. But we were up. A bottle of California rosé, half-finished, was buried in the sand next to us. We'd passed the bottle back and forth to each other like teenagers. We were laughing indulgently, laughing the laugh that only comes from good girlfriends who are intimate with each other's histories.

Joy had had to cajole her husband into coming. It's a big trip, he had said, sighing. No kidding. But my friend — she was not one to give up on me. Her name is, fittingly, a synonym for unbridled pleasure. My friend and her daughters worked on him, and he finally succumbed to all the gentle coercion. When he arrived in Maui, he fell in love with the sea turtles. *I can't get enough of them! They are everywhere! Minelle, have you seen them? They are fantastic! They are all over the beach near the condo!* He got up early in the morning, fascinated by them all, spent hours watching them. To this day, whenever he sees me, he reminds me of the magic of the turtles.

As Joy passed the bottle to me and I took a swig, I noticed my stained white North Face polar fleece jacket lying next to me. The jacket was old and tattered. I still have it. I don't know why I keep it. Actually, that's not true. Of course I know why. I had been wearing that jacket when Mary Lynn's ten-year-old daughter leaned her head on my shoulder with so much affection that it broke my heart. That was why.

That girl is now twenty-three, I think. Graduated from college. Working in Toronto. They all grow up, even when we remember them stuck in time.

Back in Vancouver, I unpacked. I pulled out the fleece jacket from my suitcase, along with my striped blue and white bikini, our wedding certificate and the requisite silly souvenirs. When I shook the jacket out, I was showered with grains of pristine white sand. It reminded me of the sugar granules falling on my head, blessing Bruce and me that day on the beach.

I could hear my mom's gold bangles clinking on her wrist.

Dalhousie

This might be the most important story. I've been saving it for you.

Shortly after Roundhouse shut down, I headed to Halifax for yet another job interview, this time at Dalhousie University. I stumbled into the Lord Nelson Hotel after the long-haul flight, unpacked my suitcase and fell asleep quickly, knowing the next day would be full of hard and harrowing interviews. Now me, the one getting interviewed.

The next morning, just as the sun slowly sifted in through the blinds, I woke up abruptly, sensing a bodily presence in the room.

I opened my eyes fully and there she was — my mom perched on the side of the bed. She smiled at me lovingly. I don't recall exactly what she was wearing, but I do remember her beatific expression. She gestured to me to sit up, and I did. She embraced me slowly and so, so warmly and said quietly in my ear, "You will get this job, Muni. You will."

I held on tight, not wanting to break the spell. My face buried in her neck, I could smell her favourite Tea Rose perfume. I just told you that I don't really remember what she was wearing, but that isn't exactly true. I know she was sporting a sea-coloured scarf that I had bought her years ago, silk and shot through with gold and silver, gently tied around her neck.

I thought, *Don't leave! Stay! Stay!* I willed her to stay, to never leave. I didn't know if she could hear me, but I didn't care. I just wanted to hold on to her as long as I could. I didn't feel the need to ask her a million questions. I didn't feel the need to speak to her. I just wanted to be with her, in that moment, and hold on tight.

The seconds ticked by, far too fast, and in the next moment, I thought I could hear my phone ring. It broke the spell. I said out loud, "No, no — don't go!" but her presence started to fade. I willed the phone to stop ringing. I asked her without words to stay.

But slowly, slowly, like fading smoke in a quiet room, she disappeared.

I looked at the clock. Five a.m.

I walked to the interview a few hours later as if in a daze, replaying her visit in my mind over and over. The interview questions, while tough, were ones I could easily handle. In fact, I was so sure of myself that at one point, I said, irritated, "Look, I know you're searching for the unicorn for this position. You will not find it. I am the closest you will get." The recruiter smirked at this response, gave me a wink after I said it. My mind was still on her scarf and the scent of my mother's perfume.

Before I left for the airport, I got the call offering me the job.

Was her visit a dream? Or did it really happen?

The questions don't matter, not those ones anyway.

I didn't really need to know the answer.

The experience was the answer.

The Boss, Now

When I was offered the job at Dalhousie, Bruce's university in Vancouver promptly created a position for me so as to not lose him. We finally had jobs together — a minor miracle.

I resigned almost immediately from my job at University of Toronto Scarborough, where they had generously been holding my position for me. When I started at my new university, I was told that I could work with PhD students, maybe even teach a graduate class in addition to my undergraduate classes.

I happened to know someone who was applying to various PhD programs. I'd tried to coax a few of my friends into taking him as one of their students, but they already had their allotted crew and shrugged, saying, *Sorry, not this year* or *His work's not really in my area.* I told them he was solid, that he got straight As in his master's, that he was really ready. But nothing seemed to be panning out.

I dialed his number, cleared my throat and posed this one last question to the person who'd taught me that truth requires the interrogative: "Would you want to work with me as your supervisor for your PhD?"

And in the split second before Don replied, I already knew the answer.

Found

_____

Remember I said I couldn't find my mother's recipe for *khao-swe* anywhere?

While I was writing this to you, I found it.

I was in Toronto seven years after she died. I had dragged Cole with me, knowing I had to finally sort through her storage locker. My cousins had rescued me, taken Cole to Centre Island, to frolic at the amusement park and go on the log ride, giving me a window to clean out her things.

That's when I found it — it was in a box of waterlogged books. She had scrawled the recipe in one of my old journals, just as I'd thought. And just like her, the recipe was adorned with beauty. It was as lovely as I remembered, with all its curlicues and doodles.

My mother may have lost her ability to speak, but her voice lives on in all these different ways — including in objects both lost and found.

Extraction

"It's a good thing we have our own secret language," Cole said in the bathtub, as he lathered himself with peppermint soap, making whirly bubbles that skimmed the surface of the water. "Otherwise we wouldn't be able to speak now."

He was now four.

You can't speak to Nana anymore, right, Mama?

Yes, junam, *I can speak to her — but she can't speak back to me.*

I had just had dental surgery, an unexpected procedure that began with an aching tooth and led to the removal of my right back molar. The Iranian dentist — again, Iranian — with his wrinkly eyes and slight accent, told me that there was no other choice if I wanted to rid myself of the infection forever.

"It will keep coming back," he said. "You can keep taking antibiotics, dealing with it on the surface, or just take it out, so that it can't come back at all."

I gripped the hygienist's hand so tightly I was afraid I would break her delicate bones. I heard the cracking of enamel as the dentist roughly tore the molar out of my mouth. He held it up and showed me the roots. "All gone now," he said.

When I got home, my mouth so padded with blood-soaked gauze that I could hardly speak, my son looked at me and said, "Mama, I will take care of you." He put his hand to his forehead, tapped his fingers there and, even though he had a voice, said the secret words we use to speak about love.

I can't write them here. I promised I never would, and I never will.

The Visit

This next story was gifted to me. And now I am gifting it to you.

Will you cherish it, please? Will you promise to hold it close to your chest, over your beating breast, or place it gently under your pillow?

Here it is.

My mother told me a story when I was about nine. She said after her father died, she was saying her Namaz one night on the floor of her bedroom when her father suddenly appeared, perched on the bed, beside her. The image was plain as day. He was there.

He said to her, "Everything will be okay," and then he slowly disappeared into the ether, and from that moment on, she believed him.

I always thought she dreamed it, or that she had made the story up, offering it to a child as a way to provide comfort.

But now I know better. I know it actually happened.

I still think a lot about revolutions. The importance of them, to be sure, and what they can teach us. How every moment can be a quiet revolution in thinking, if only we allow it. But I also think about the revolutions so present in my life: my mom's experience of her father visiting her, my experience of my mother visiting me, both figures so precariously perched on the sides of our beds. The rotation of the connection, the repetition of the revolution of it all.

What I take away from both visits is the same. The message being: I am here, I am here with you.

Hear me whisper loudly in your ear.

Hear me tell you that I am here, with you.

MY MOTHER'S KHAO-SWE RECIPE

Ingredients

Onions

Garlic

Ginger

1 ½ cups chicken thighs, uncooked, chopped in ½ inch pieces

Haldi (turmeric)

1 can coconut milk

Egg noodles

Three boiled eggs, peeled and sliced

Dhania (cilantro), for topping

Lemons, for topping

Dried red chili flakes, for topping

Fish sauce, for topping

Scallions, for topping

Directions

Fry onions till glazed and slightly browned. Taste one. It should taste slightly burnt, look dark on the edges. Add garlic and ginger until fragrant. Remove from pan. Add chicken until cooked. Add turmeric until chicken is coloured slightly orange. Add coconut milk and bring to a boil. Meanwhile, boil a pot of water separately. Add the egg noodles. Cook until softened. When drained, plate the noodles in each bowl. Then top each nest of noodles with the *khao-swe* sauce. Make sure you add a few slices of egg, and *dhania*. I like a lot of lemon squeezed on the top, and a handful of red chili flakes, but do whatever your taste prefers. Enjoy knowing that this is a dish that has been passed down from generation to generation and make it your own by adding various toppings that make you happy, the way my own mother did.

Acknowledgements

"For last year's words belong to last year's language
And next year's words await another voice.
[...]
What we call the beginning is often the end
And to make an end is to make a beginning."

— T.S. ELIOT, "Little Gidding"

It feels odd to write my own acknowledgements when I have spent so much time scrutinizing other people's acknowledgements for clues in order to book guests on my show! But now the roles are reversed and I am tasked with trying to thank so many. This book was penned when I was both grieving my mother and trying to make sense of the world post-pandemic. I owe many people a debt of gratitude for their patience and kindness.

There are two writers I want to single out who nourished me with their friendship as I stumbled through this project — Jenny Heijun Wills and David Chariandy. They are both midwives for this book, while all errors are mine alone.

I met Heijun while on a fellowship at the Banff Centre. I heard her read from what would become her memoir, *Older Sister. Not Necessarily Related*. I was blessed in that she would later call me friend.

Our relationship has been life-sustaining; she is not only an expert on telling me where to find the best face cleanser and lip liner, she also provided nuanced and careful critique on early drafts. Thank you so much, Heijun.

This book would not exist if not for the extraordinary generosity of the award-winning writer David Chariandy. Our families met serendipitously at The Naam one morning. At breakfast's end, he invited us to dinner that night. Who does that? Only David. This chance encounter led to several happy meetings, including our families celebrating our children's birthdays together.

I know I am not alone in experiencing David's astonishing kindness. But what David did for me feels unprecedented. When this book was but a talk that I was going to present at Dalhousie, a morose and meandering meditation on failure, I tentatively shared it with David. As we sat eating lunch at Tractor in Kitsilano, he said, with that lovely laugh of his, "Minelle, I think you might have a book here." I kept those words close to my heart and heeded them when I thought about giving up. Thank you, David, there is no one like you.

David read over early drafts, offered support, encouragement and warm introductions that eventually led to my connection to my extremely talented, courageous and brilliant agent, Stephanie Sinclair. I'll never forget the steadfast faith that Stephanie had in this project. She saw what I was trying to do, and helped me meet and eventually acquire a deal with my editor, Melanie Tutino.

The day I received my offer was the same day I quit an administrative post at my university. I couldn't help but see the offer as a sign, of course. That first conversation with Melanie convinced me in mere minutes that I was working with my dream editor. Meticulous down to the last punctuation point, Melanie has that rare gift to see both the small and big picture; to listen to what I didn't say on the page and to coax the little sparrows out of me to make sure my own voice sang. I couldn't have imagined a better editor. Or anyone I'd rather sip on a glass of rosé with at the Granville Island Hotel. It's a rare and wonderful combination and one that I hope to experience again!

The entire team at Doubleday Canada has been wonderful to work with: getting to know Megan Kwan and her stylistic attention to detail has been terrific; as has the work of copyeditor Crissy Calhoun and proofreader Alison Strobel, who caught all sorts of things I absolutely missed. I also want to thank my publicist Chalista Andadari.

So many friends and mentors provided support by reading earlier bits of drafts. In no particular order, these individuals listened to me ramble about the book. Thank you so much, Ninan Abraham, Kamal Al-Solaylee, Emily Andrew, Ron Buliung, Paul Bramadat, Hollay Ghadery, Don Gillmor, Hamlin Grange, William Green, Josh Greenberg, Ed Henderson, Frances Henry, Stuart Horwitz, Tajja Isen, Shelina Kassam, Chelene Knight, Christine Lai, Meera Lakhani-Winsor, Kirk LaPointe, Lucia Lorenzi, Eternity Martis, Rebecca and Theo Morrocco, Cynthia Reyes, Leonie Sandercock, Emi Sasagawa, Risa Schwartz, Sarita Srivastava, Julietta Singh, Archana Sridhar, Timothy Taylor, Jean Teillet, Justin Tse, Jasmin Zine and Mary Zournazi. And I am grateful to my new agent, Ron Eckel, whom I met after Stephanie left to become the publisher of McClelland & Stewart. I'm sure there are others I have left off this list inadvertently. If so, forgive me!

Thank you to previous editors and publications that gave my early work a home, including *The Walrus*, *This Magazine*, *Maisonneuve*, *carte blanche* and *VICE*. I want to especially thank those editors who were patient with me and helped make my work better: Carine Abouseif, Emma Cleary, Natasha Grzincic, Madi Haslam and Tara-Michelle Ziniuk. Thanks for taking a chance on me.

When I was at the CBC as a junior producer and going through a bit of a hard time, Gail Gallant, a senior producer, novelist and memoirist said just the right thing to make me feel better. More than twenty years later, when I was in a different predicament, she would offer me solace again. Thank you, Gail, for always being in my corner and reminding me to let my light shine.

My close circle of girlfriends are the mothers and daughters of my heart who make me laugh until my belly aches. I can't thank enough Karen Campbell, Joylyn S. Chai (magic), Sylvia Fuller, Carrianne Leung (BBFF!), Sheryl Lightfoot, Marichka Melnyk, Brenda Nadjiwan, Shirley Nakata (deviator #1), Roshni Narain (deviator #2), Emily Pohl-Weary, Juanita Sundberg, Jean Teillet and Mary Lynn Young. A special thank you to Maisie Wong, who told me many years ago while I was but an undergraduate at Dalhousie: "Minelle, one day you will write a book." You were right, Maise! Thanks for having faith in me when I didn't.

There are many public intellectuals whose work has sustained me over the years and from whom I draw in this manuscript. The names and titles of those works are listed on my website (minellemahtani.com) but I wanted to do a special shoutout to those friends I specifically speak about here: Sonja Boon, Candis Callison, Alicia Elliott, Katherine McKittrick, Jean Teillet and Mary Lynn Young. Thank you for the richness of your intellectual endeavours. Your writing has indelibly shaped me. I am grateful to Robyn Grant-Moran who offered editorial guidance on an early draft.

My students are my best teachers. I have learned so much from them over the years. I am so grateful to past students in my GRSJ 101 class, Risk, Relation, Revolution and Repair, who have now graduated. A special thanks to Lulu Jama, Abigaelle Normand and Abril Soewarso-Rivera. After hearing the story about my mother, my former student Katalina Hilton always sends me a little note every Mother's Day. Thank you, Katalina. I'd also like to thank the following students who have brought much joy to my life while teaching me, too: Alyana Amadeo, Emily Elizabeth Evans, Simran Garcha, Emilee Guilfoyle, Lila Jones, Karla Jubaily, Harvir Lochab, Eiko Masutani,

Tessa Mok, Bella Nelstrop, Gurnoor Powar, Aryana Raj, Charlie Sutherland, Peach Trippell and Kennice Wong.

The students in my CDST 450 class provided great intellectual nourishment. Thanks to Will Shelling, Isabelle Espanol, Naeemah Shah, Xin Wang, Jasmine Manango and Zihao Zhang for taking the risk to write with me. You offered me a model of a constellation of care.

The stunning illustrations in the book are courtesy of Daisy Osberg. Daisy was a student in my GRSJ 101 class and in one of her assignments, she had offered some artwork. I was so amazed by her talent that I asked her to read my manuscript and she generously provided these beautiful sketches. Daisy, you are so talented. I hope we can work together again someday — that is, if other authors don't snap you up (and if you are someone who is interested, do I have a contact for you!).

It's not often that family will support a memoir that unveils complex family secrets and stories. But my family is not like all other families. I am fortunate that my brother, Ray (Reza) Mahtani not only tolerated my decision to pursue this deep dive into our family's intimacies but also cheered me on. I owe you, Ray.

My cousin Zhaleh read over a draft and offered feedback. I'm grateful for her love and kindness. I am lucky to have some terrific writers in my family who also read over drafts — Erica Cardwell, my cousin-in-law who encouraged me, and my cousin Anise Vance, whose own novel inspired me to reach to new heights.

I feel privileged to have married into a family of people whom I not only love, but like. My mother-in-law is one of those people who see everything and says little when it comes to offering advice or passing judgment. She's the best. Thank you for always offering me grace, Rosalyn. So many other family members deserve a shout-out: Carolina, my brilliant and wonderful cousin-in-law, her husband, R.J., their daughters, Isabella and Mia; as well as my family across the pond in France: Kevin, Elisabeth and Thomas. Thomas survived an internship at Roundhouse with me years ago. And my sister-in-law, Andrea, who told me that the book made her laugh and cry, and my niece, Jessica Myers, whom I admire greatly.

Don Shafer. I could never have imagined that you and I would be where we are now, but of course I know that it could not be any other way. I cherish our relationship. As I witness you come close to finishing your dissertation, it's been such a joy to work with you and be your supervisor. You read over drafts of this memoir and always told me, *This is your story — not mine — it must be true to you.* Thank you for trusting in me, Don. Not everyone would have been open to me telling this story. I can't wait to call you Dr. Shafer.

Sherene Razack has always been there for me. Over many glasses of wine at Bar Mercurio, she would school me on what I needed to get tenure and never minced words when it came to critiquing my work, and always did this with laughter and generosity. I admire her commitment to her political practice and adore her family. Thank you for always being there for me, Sherene. Now can I come visit you in LA again?

I have had many teachers who guided me while I worked on early drafts. I took a course with the talented writer Lindsay Wong during the pandemic. Lindsay's commitment to mentoring students is unparalleled. Thanks so much, Lindsay, for all your advice. I was lucky to be taught by Terese Marie Mailhot at Tin House. When I first heard that I had gotten into her workshop, I was thrilled. It turned out that one of my all-time favourite writers would be a gifted teacher too. Thank you, Terese. Working with Heidi Durrow at Hedgebrook made an already beautiful geography on Whidbey Island even more exquisite and powerful. Thank you for seeing me, Heidi. And although I have known Kyo Maclear for years now since writing my own academic book on mixed race identity, it was through my time learning from her at Banff that I benefitted from her teaching.

I want to thank the Banff Centre for Art and Creativity and in particular the participants in the Centering Ourselves workshop for an outstanding learning experience. I felt honoured to share space with all of you. I am also grateful to the Hedgebrook Writer's Retreat for two productive stays and to the Tin House 2021 Winter Fellowship.

The pandemic was hard for everyone. For me, someone who glows in the company of others, basking in their light, I felt far too much darkness most days. What saved me were two things. The first was the love of a beautiful new puppy in the form of a sheepadoodle named Pluto. Pluto's playful ways made me feel alive again. Pluto also introduced me to a new circle of friends and made a cold city much warmer through our daily trips to the dog park. At our informal evening gatherings in Cedar Cottage, while our dogs frolicked, I met and still meet a constellation of beautiful people — and dogs — who make me smile every day. Thank you so much, Anita and Jason and Kayla; Sakis and Esther; Masee; Shaun; Kayla; Brian, Andrea and Arlo; Cathy; Sebastien and Kyrani! Kyrani gets double thanks because she also took my author photo.

And of course our dogs also deserve serious thanks too — big scritches to Pluto, Hiro, Otis, Dapper, Hector, Pax, Roza, Puff and Indy. Pictures of dogs on request. Because who doesn't need more pictures of dogs?

This book is dedicated to my friend Ing Wong-Ward. What I did not say at the start was that Ing died in 2019. I miss her all the time. I'm lucky that her daughter is my godchild and I am so in awe of the vivacious spirit and joy that is Zhenmei Wong-Ward. I love you, Zhenmei, and am always proud of you.

Finally, I'm grateful to my little family. This book would not have been possible without Bruce, my kind, curly-haired husband who watched his wife wander away weekends to a nearby hotel to feverishly write during the last few months of this project and yet he never complained. Thank you, honey. And of course, my always funny and terrifically clever son Cole who read over much of the book and even offered some pseudonyms! I love you so much — for the person you are, and the person you are becoming. I say to you now our secret words, but only to you, always.

Permissions

The lines from *Small Cures*, copyright © 2020 by Della Hicks-Wilson. Used by permission of Della Hicks-Wilson.

The lines from "reconnaissance," copyright © 2007 by Rita Wong. Used by permission of Rita Wong.

The Rumi quote, copyright © 2023 by Rumi Network. Used by permission of Rumi Network, www.Rumi.net.

The lines from "Bosom Stones: Tomb for Mother" by Yadollah Roya'i from *Belonging: New Poetry by Iranians Around the World*, edited and translated by Niloufar Talebi, published by North Atlantic Books, copyright © 2008 by Niloufar Talebi. Reprinted by permission of North Atlantic Books.

The lines from *That's What Grandmas Do!* by Alarie Tennille, copyright © 2015 by Hallmark Licensing, LLC.

The lines from "A Litany for Survival," copyright © 1978 by Audre Lorde, from *The Collected Poems of Audre Lorde* by Audre Lorde. Used by permission of W. W. Norton & Company, Inc.